HELPING STUDENTS WITH HOMEWORK

WITHDRAWN

Janice Amos Wood, Ph.D.
University of North Florida

Kendall/Hunt
Publishing Company
Dubuque, Iowa

D1508436

Dedication

**To my husband, Lowell, and my mother,
Molly, who have encouraged me to
write this book. To my children,
Joel and Courtney, who have
inspired me.**

LB
1048
W66

Ronald Williams Library
Northeastern Illinois University

BT GAB 3/23/88

Copyright © 1987 Kendall/Hunt Publishing Company

Library of Congress Catalog Card Number: 87-81474

ISBN 0-8403-4404-X

All rights reserved. No part of this publication may be reproduced,
stored in a retrieval system, or transmitted, in any form or by any
means, electronic, mechanical, photocopying, recording, or otherwise,
without the prior written permission of the copyright owner.

Printed in the United States of America
10 9 8 7 6 5 4 3 2 1

Contents

Preface

The teacher today is responsible for teaching many subject areas. Because of this renewed interest in the basic academic skills, teachers regularly assign homework to provide opportunities for students to practice skills learned in school and explore new areas of study. Formal homework assignments usually begin in fourth grade and continue through grade twelve. Generally, homework is given four times a week and takes approximately one hour to complete. Recently, many school systems have implemented programs that offer homework assistance to students after school hours. There are many homework assistance programs currently in operation throughout the country. Many students have homework assignments with which they need help. The students who are experiencing skill difficulty often require individual attention. Homework assistance programs offer regular, individual academic assistance to students who encounter problems in the successful completion of school assignments.

This book was written to offer the teacher strategies for assisting students with after school assignments. Chapter 1 defines homework and reviews the types of homework teachers assign. Chapter 2 lays the groundwork for instructing individual students. The chapter focuses on effective ways to help the student learn the subject matter. Chapters 3 and 4 provide steps for planning a positive learning environment. A supportive climate has positive effects on learning and the information in these two chapters offers practical ways for teachers to implement a learning climate that is warm and reinforcing. The chapters discuss communication strategies that may be utilized by teachers to improve listening, understanding, memory and concentration. Chapter 5 provides steps for assigning homework, organizing the assignments and managing time. Chapter 6 was written for students. It outlines step-by-step study methods that students can review and use. Students who attempt to refine study habits are more likely to comprehend the material and generally do better in school.

The material in this book will provide useful information to teachers who want to help students successfully complete class and homework assignments.

1 *Homework in Schools Today*

Since the first school opened its doors, the subject of homework has been debated regarding its effectiveness. However, most educators feel that homework has several useful functions. Homework prepares students for future assignments and allows for practice sessions and reinforcement of skills learned. It also provides for extension and enrichment of subject matter covered in class by integrating many skills. Homework is not just an activity to keep students busy at home. It is for all students, and should be thought of as a positive learning experience which offers students a sense of accomplishment and provides opportunities to practice skills and explore new areas of study.

Although homework has long been an accepted tradition in our schools, it has moved to the educational forefront in the past decade. More recently, there has been widespread interest in raising school standards with increased attention on basic skills and academic achievement. As a result of recent media emphasis and exposure, parents, administrators and teachers have a renewed interest in the issue of increased homework and higher expectations for completion of homework assignments. Homework is viewed by parents, educators and students as a means toward academic excellence and future success in school in general.

Homework encourages and enriches school experiences through related home activities. It acquaints parents with what their children are learning in school. A bond between the school and home can be important to a student's success in school.

Definition of Homework

Homework is an activity or a series of activities students are assigned to do on their own time. It is expected to be completed at home, and is used by the classroom teacher as a means of enriching skills learned, preparing for future assignments or enriching specified topic areas. Ideally, homework assignments provide logical extensions of class work and should fit the individual abilities and interests of the students.

Types of Homework

Recent polls show that approximately eight-five per cent of teachers favor the use of homework with students in grades three through twelve. The assignment of homework also is favored by parents and is frequently mentioned as a way to raise standards and public opinions about our schools. Teachers usually assign homework four days a week which means that students are completing assignments daily, since many of the assignments are long term assignments.

Homework can be categorized into three types of assignments: practice, preparation, and enrichment.

Practice Type Homework

Practice homework is by far the most common type and accounts for the majority of homework assigned. The purpose of practice assignments is to provide students with opportunities to reinforce, through practice, newly acquired skills learned in the classroom. Practice exercises reinforce the mastery of skills usually in the areas of math, language arts, science, history and social studies. Often, practice type assignments are long, dull and uninteresting. Some students may be unable to complete them because they have not mastered specific skills in the classroom. However, practice type exercises that are appropriate to the students' individual capacities are worthwhile.

Practice type exercises may include reading, drill, memorization and writing. Examples include practicing a specific mathematical operation such as multiplication by completing practice items of multiplication problems. Another assignment might include memorizing the names of state capitals.

Preparation Type Homework

Preparation type homework assignments are given to prepare students for future classroom lessons. These assignments are often daily reading assignments given at the completion of a lesson. The students are asked to read specific chapters in the text, to learn facts, to answer questions at the end of the chapter, or to draw inferences or conclusions. An important consideration in assigning preparation type homework is the reading ability of the students. Students who do not read well will have difficulty completing exercises which require independent reading.

Another common type preparation assignment involves preparing for tests. The teacher generally acquaints students with the specific areas that the test will cover and suggests a variety of study strategies to assist the student in preparing for the test.

Enrichment Type Homework

Enrichment type assignments are given to determine if the students can integrate and transfer newly learned skills to new situations. These assignments are usually written, long-term projects which are student produced or created. The assignment involves the students in the identification of the project as well as in the method of investigation. Enrichment type assignments can be completed individually or in small groups and usually are extensions of classroom topic areas. Examples of enrichment projects would include science projects, book reports and research projects.

Homework can involve reading, writing,memorizing or drill and can be either short term assignments or long term assignments. Recent research supports the importance of carefully planned homework. Homework stimulates initiative, responsibility and self-direction. Students themselves prefer homework that gives them an opportunity to use their skills in problem solving activities.

Today's school curriculum covers so many subject areas that homework is sometimes necessary to allow children more practice sessions to reinforce learning, to help prepare students for future lessons and to enrich and integrate many skill areas. Although the amount of homework appears to be increasing, the three basic types of homework are still regularly assigned. Most homework supports classroom work and usually includes a review of previously learned material.

Basic Concepts of Homework

Although over the years we have found shifts of emphasis regarding homework, it has recently enjoyed a renewed interest by schools. Teachers have regularly assigned homework in various subject areas. There has been a broad range of opinions, and studies regarding the value of homework have reported conflicting results. While a few studies indicated that homework had minimal impact on student achievement, other studies suggested that students who were given regular, definite, individualized assignments had more significant achievement gains and higher test scores than students who had no homework. Generally, average and below average students who were able to complete homework assignments showed higher achievement gains than did above average students although both groups showed gains. Teacher feedback and specific comments on completed homework helped all students with achievement.

There are no clear cut answers regarding homework although parents, students and teachers all accept home study as part of the educational process. Successful homework assignments involve students, parents and teachers all working together. Research studies have found a positive relationship between time spent on appropriate homework assignments and good school achievement. Homework also promotes positive relations among parents, teachers and students.

Advantages of Homework

- Reinforces skills learned in school
- Enriches the curriculum
- Prepares students for class work
- Develops self-discipline, responsibility and independence
- Develops study habits
- Promotes school achievement
- Allows for completion of unfinished work
- Develops a cooperative partnership between home and school
- Maintains student interest in the learning process
- Prepares students for future study

3

ments that are dull and mechanical often encourage students to "copy" each
ework. Copying defeats the purpose of homework and usually has a detrimental
eπect on the learning process. As students advance through the grades, the practice of
copying homework increases. The reasons students give for copying include forgetting
assignments and being unable to complete the assignments.

Complaints about Homework

- Assignments too long and uninteresting
- School day already long enough
- Students lack skills to complete assignments
- No academic assistance available
- Leaves little time for leisure activities
- Disrupts home life
- Causes stress and anxiety
- Poor study environments
- Unavailable resources to complete homework

Amount of Homework Assigned

There doesn't appear to be a consensus on how much homework should be assigned.
Regular, formal homework usually begins in the fourth grade although many first, second
and third grade students are assigned informal homework exercises. As students progress
from elementary school to high school, the amount of homework increases and the amount
of time needed to complete assignments also increases. Furthermore, the time students spend
on homework has increased over the years. As a result of excessive homework, many
students have complained of fatigue. Some schools have adopted a system where students are
given assignments in only two subjects a day. Students and parents report positive reactions
to the structured amount of homework and the time spent completing it.

Parents' Point of View

When surveyed, most parents favored homework and felt it helped achieve better
grades and developed self-discipline, independence and improved study skills. All parents
agreed that homework helped bridge the gap between home and school, although little
research supports the notion that cooperative partnerships between the home and school
promote student achievement (Walberg,1984). The parents who did not favor homework felt

that the school day was long enough for students to complete academic assignments and felt too much emphasis was placed on successfully completing regular homework assignments by classroom teachers. Many of the parents who did not favor homework did not understand either the school policy or the educators' policy on homework. Recently completed surveys found that although the majority of teachers assign homework, most school districts do not have a written policy concerning specific homework procedures.

Most parents favor regular, nightly practice type homework assignments, while most teachers favor enrichment type assignments as well as assignments which might take several days to complete. While parents favor homework, more recently they have urged school systems to assign homework based on individual student needs and have urged moderation in the amount of homework assigned. Many felt that the development of leisure time activities was hindered because of the amount of homework regularly assigned. All parents preferred homework that could be successfully completed in a reasonable time period, and assignments that could be clearly understood by the students. Many parents responded that homework should maintain student interest in learning, not discourage it. Parents who were involved with their children's educational progress felt that homework prepared students for future study.

Parents differed about their attitudes regarding helping their children with homework. Some parents welcomed the opportunity to work regularly with their children, while others did not. Some of the most frequently stated reasons for not helping their children were that parents were unable to assist because of their own work schedules or because they were unable to understand the assignments. The parents who did not work with their children felt it was a waste of time to try to assist their children because they did not have the skills necessary for the completion of the assignment. Parents, as well as students, felt that more instruction on how to study and prepare for assignments and tests would be beneficial.

Educators' Point of View

The practice of assigning homework has remained unchanged over the past fifty years. Assigning formal homework usually begins in the fourth grade and continues through grade twelve. Recent surveys have found that eighty-five per cent of teachers favor assigning homework on a regular basis. Homework is usually given four times a week and takes between one hour and one and a half hours to complete daily. While sixty-two percent of all homework is assigned in math, language arts homework follows closely behind with twenty-two percent. (Wood, 1986)

Some of the reasons teachers assign homework include teaching independence, developing self-discipline, enriching the curriculum, offering additional skill practice and developing closer home and school relationships. Other reasons cited were teaching thinking skills and providing opportunities for creative endeavors. By far the most common reason teachers assign homework is to reinforce basic skills. Homework provides practice by giving the student opportunities to complete activities within specified skill areas. Most students need more than one or two practice exercises to learn a skill. Because of time constraints, distractions and disruptions in the classroom, many students are unable to complete all assignments in school, therefore requiring time at home to successfully complete the assignments.

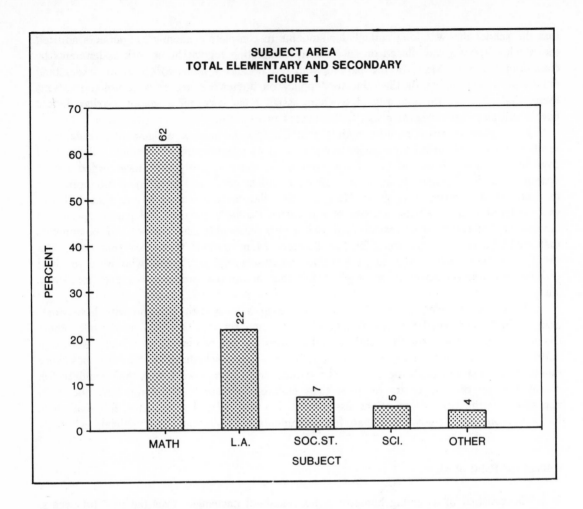

SUBJECT AREA
TOTAL ELEMENTARY AND SECONDARY
FIGURE 1

Although a significant number of all teachers favor the use of homework, more homework is given when the teacher perceives that the class has above average academic ability. Recent studies (Azimi and Madhere,1982, Purkey and Smith, 1982, Green and Brown, 1983) found that effective teachers produced higher student achievers. Other studies have found that students in private schools are often better achievers than those in public schools because they receive more homework and get more individual attention not only from their teachers, but also from their parents. It might be said that individual attention could well account for higher achievement both in school and in the home than the actual assignment of homework. These studies suggest that individual attention rather than the actual assignment of homework could account for higher achievement both in school and at home.

Studies dealing with the correlation between homework and academic achievement have not been consistent. It is generally agreed that the amount of homework increases significantly as a student progresses through school and that the amount of time a student spends on homework assignments has increased over the past thirty years. Recent studies have indicated that correctly completed homework is positively correlated to higher test scores, specifically in the area of math computational skills. Teachers who carefully checked and graded homework reported that their students usually completed the assignments because they knew the results impacted on final grades. When homework was assigned and completed, students who completed the homework appeared to do better on short, daily quizzes. On the other hand, some studies reported that achievement was not affected when homework was completed. Homework that was carefully assigned at the appropriate academic levels of the students seems to help in improving achievement. No studies indicate that homework has a negative effect. (Suydam, 1985)

Students' Point of View

Recent surveys of elementary and secondary students have found that students generally felt that homework assignments are necessary and helped them improve their grades and do better on exams. Although many students stated that they didn't like homework, almost all students said they did some kind of homework fairly regularly. Students with a reasonable amount of homework had little objections to doing it if they saw in it value for classwork. Students want homework that gives them a chance to use their own initiative and provide opportunities to enrich school learning. Many students felt the purpose of homework was to review class work and didn't study unless a project was due or a test was forthcoming. Seventy-five percent of students felt that homework in math, English, social studies and science helped them achieve better grades in those subject areas. Many students felt that homework specifically helped them achieve better grades in math computational skills. (Kerzic,1966)

Students who do well in school are more likely to complete homework than students who are having academic difficulties or who have repeated a grade. It is these students who are not learning the skills necessary to complete homework. While the average and above average students ask teachers for explanations when they do not understand, the less able students usually do not ask for assistance. Successful students reported that they liked to be assigned work that provided opportunities to research topics of interest, to solve problems, to read good literature and to do experiments. They objected to assignments given as "busywork" and assignments that were long, mechanical exercises requiring memorization. Ninety percent of all students reported that they need assistance at least some of the time with their homework assignments.

Several programs that assisted students with homework assignments reported that of all students requesting assistance, twenty-eight percent of the requests were in elementary math and thirty-three per cent of the requests were in secondary math. Elementary language arts students requested assistance thirteen percent of the time, while secondary language arts students required assistance eight per cent of the time. (Wood, 1986)

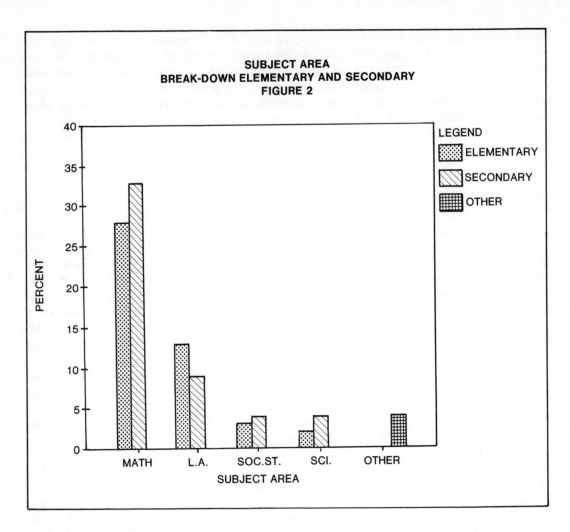

**SUBJECT AREA
BREAK-DOWN ELEMENTARY AND SECONDARY
FIGURE 2**

LEGEND
ELEMENTARY
SECONDARY
OTHER

PERCENT

SUBJECT AREA

MATH   L.A.   SOC.ST.   SCI.   OTHER

Student Expectations

While most students expect homework, they stated that homework was more manageable when they had a clear understanding of the skills necessary to complete the assignment and support and resource materials available to them. The students also reported that they needed a quiet place to study without interruptions. If assignments require outside resources, the student should have access to the materials required. For example, teachers often allow for library research time during regular school hours to acquaint students with the library in general and how to locate resources and information in the center. The teacher should not assume that students have access to materials such as newspapers, maps and dictionaries outside the school. Since most students study at home, positive study conditions are important. A home study area should be designated, free of distractions, for regular use by the students. It was found that even when students understood the assignment and the conditions were positive, most students needed assistance with homework on a regular basis.

More able students who were assigned homework tended to make higher grades than students who were not assigned homework. Average and below average students who were not assigned homework did not do as well as students who were assigned homework. When students did not have home study, they often enrolled in evening classes and spent increased time in sports, hobbies and other interests. Parents reported that they preferred appropriate amounts of individualized assignments rather than no homework.

One of the most common students complaints about homework was that teachers failed to give adequate feedback. However, students reacted favorably to teachers who thoroughly explained assignments, made comments about errors and suggested improvements. Other complaints stated by students were that the exercises were dull and mechanical and that the assignments were too long. Students felt that many teachers had unrealistic ideas about the length of time required to complete assignments. Thus, when excessive homework minimizes or eliminates social experiences and recreation, it does not meet the basic needs of students and negatively affects the students' feelings about the educational process.

Time Spent Completing Homework

The amount of time students spent on homework varied greatly in responses not only from students, but from parents as well as teachers. According to responses from students, the time taken to complete homework ranged from no-time to four hours daily. An average daily completion time was sixty-two minutes. (Kerzie, 1966) Almost always, the total time it took students to complete homework was higher than teacher estimates. Teachers and students both agreed that homework should be assigned on a regular basis and should range in completion time from one hour for short term assignments to two hours for long term assignments:

- Fifty-four percent are overnight assignments

- Twenty-one percent are of several days' duration

- Twenty-five percent are of more than a week's duration

Other studies have found different time ranges in the elementary and the secondary levels. In grades one through three, teachers generally believed that school work should be completed during the day and that after school a student might elect to read books or participate in a "special" project relating to school work. After grade school the amount of time spent in homework varied greatly.

- Grades 4, 5, 6   Sixty minutes a day, four days a week

- Grades 6, 7, 8   Sixty-two minutes a day, four days a week

- Grade 9   Thirty-three percent of the students spent no time on homework; fifteen percent spent two hours a day, four days a week

- Grades 10, 11   Ten hours a week

Since many seniors in high school are involved in extra curricular activities that require extensive time and social interaction, most studies showed a decline in homework in grade twelve. The college-bound student however, reported time spent to approximate the ten hours a week reported in grades ten and eleven.

Time spent in home study competed with participation in sport activities and out-of-school activities such as jobs and hobbies for students in the secondary grades. Students who were excessively involved in non-academic activities often had negative feelings concerning homework because they were unable to complete the assignments in the allotted time. Time spent completing homework varies not only from school to school, but varies within grade levels in the same school. One teacher may assign short, daily exercises while another may assign long-term, weekly exercises.

It has been estimated that students spend an average of thirty hours a week watching television and an average of only four hours a week on homework. The college-bound student appeared to spend the most time on homework, with the less able student spending the least amount of time on homework. Girls spent more time than boys on homework.

If schoolwork is challenging, the brighter students may spend considerable amount of time completing their assignments. The time students spend on home study depends on a number of factors. The climate of some schools may encourage academic gains and achievement by recognizing high grades through "honor rolls" or "honor clubs." Students' home environments also influence study habits according to the value the students' parents place on achievement. Parents who encourage academic performance monitor homework and encourage their children to complete it regularly and correctly.

Making the Best Out of Homework

While most school systems do not have stated homework policies, a majority of teachers, administrators and parents favor homework, and most teachers regularly assign homework. Two common problems with homework assignments are that they are often given as busywork or they require only superficial understanding. Exercises should not be mechanical, but should rather place emphasis on imagination, initiative and research. When a reasonable amount of homework is assigned, most students will have little objection to completing the assignment if they can see the value of the assignment to their classwork and to future needs.

Homework is helpful, not harmful, but it has value only if it is carefully planned by the teacher and based on individual student needs and progress. It should be interesting and relevant and provide opportunities for student direction. Consideration should be given to demands on student time outside the school environment. Excessively long homework usually has negative effects on both students and parents.

While advanced students regularly complete homework assignments, slower students are less likely to complete them, although the slower students are more likely to profit from completing their homework. All students should have opportunities to discuss with their teachers their homework assignments and problems they may encounter in completing the assignments. On the other hand, teachers should give recognition to completed homework and should systematically correct, grade and return assignments within a reasonable time frame. Homework that grows out of stimulating school experiences usually proves worthwhile endeavor. Effective strategies regarding homework assignments should be no...

- Individualize homework assignments whenever possible
- Make sure students understand assignments
- Entertain student questions regarding assignments
- Make assignments interesting and relevant
- Keep assignments short
- Evaluate and return homework
- Keep parents informed about homework
- Provide assistance to students when necessary

Homework Assistance Programs

In the past ten years, many academic homework assistance programs have become available to students in several school systems throughout the country. Most students have homework assignments in which they need assistance. Homework programs offer regular assistance to students in some school districts. Many students find homework assignments difficult to complete without some assistance from the teacher whose time for such assistance is minimal, therefore, the development of Homework Assistance Programs. The rationale for homework assistance is to provide a free source of immediate aid to students and to parents who encounter problems in the successful completion of homework assignments. (Wood, 1986)

Telephone Homework Assistance Program

The telephone assistance program is open to all students who have access to telephones. It is usually housed in a central location in a public school system. The program consists of a bank of telephones installed by the school system. The homework telephones are assigned a special telephone number that students can call after school hours to obtain help with homework assignments. The telephone program is open four nights a week, three hours a night. The telephones are manned by certified teachers who help the students or parents find solutions to their problems. Since the program is not a tutoring program, the telephone teachers do not give direct answers to the problems, but rather help the students find the answers themselves. The telephone calls usually take three to five minutes to complete.

11

Another program that helps students with their homework is called the school based assistance program. It consists of after school homework assistance and is offered at designated local schools. The school based programs are usually housed in the school media center and each center is staffed with certificated teachers. The school based program provides one-to-one assistance in all academic areas to all students who stay after school to obtain help with their homework assignments. The program is open several afternoons a week, for two hours a day, to allow students to go to their local schools and receive assistance in completing difficult homework. Another objective of the school based programs is to allow the student opportunities to visit the library after school hours to engage in independent projects or just to browse through the books, newspapers or magazines.

An analysis of data collected indicated that sixty-two percent of the requests directed to homework assistance programs concerned math; twenty-nine percent of those students had questions concerning elementary math, and thirty-three percent of the calls concerned secondary math. A total of twenty-two percent of the calls concerned English, language arts, and reading. More than half the total calls for assistance, fifty-seven percent, were from fourth, fifth, sixth, and seventh-graders. (Wood, 1986)

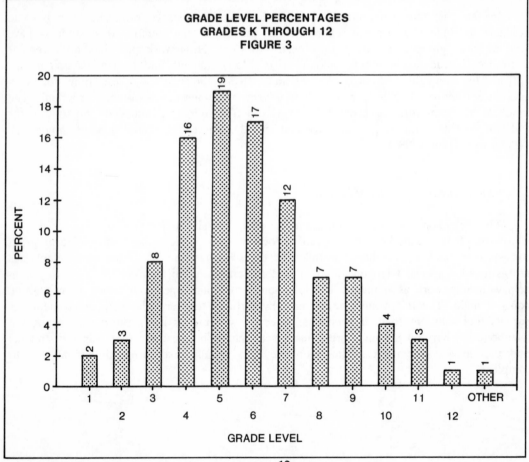

It can be concluded from the number of participants that teachers and parents desire academic assistance. It has been reported that not only students, but parents desire some kind of assistance for successful completion of homework. Because of programs like these, parents are becoming partners in their childrens' education. Students have reported overall enthusiasm and positive attitudes toward the Homework Assistance Programs.

Summary

This chapter has provided a general overview of homework in schools today. The research has repeatedly confirmed that homework is an accepted tradition in our schools. The reports confirmed that students, teachers and parents all accept homework as part of the educational process.

Teachers have regularly assigned homework in various subject areas. There has been a broad range of opinions and studies regarding the value of homework with conflicting results. While a few studies indicated that homework had minimal impact on students' achievement, it is generally agreed that students who were given regular, definite, individualized assignments had more significant achievement gains and higher test scores.

It was found that formal homework assignments usually began in fourth grade and continued through grade twelve. It is usually given four times a week and takes between one hour and one and a half hours to complete. While sixty-two percent of the homework is assigned in math, language arts homework follows closely with twenty-two percent. Homework is usually categorized into three types of assignments: practice, preparation and enrichment.

In order for homework to be beneficial to the students, it should be carefully planned by the teacher. It should be based on individual student needs, be interesting and relevant. Students should be able to see the value of homework assignments and how they relate to classwork and future needs.

2
Helping Students Complete Homework Assignments

This chapter classifies major components of instruction. Although the identified components can be used in a classroom situation, an effort has been made to focus on individual or small group instruction. Teaching should be an exciting activity. This chapter focuses on the individual student and ways to help him learn. Working with individuals or small groups of learners makes it easy to tailor teaching in terms of learner needs. When you individually tailor teaching, students have opportunities to acquire needed skills and to progress at their own pace.

Six major components of teaching dominate individual and small group instruction:

1. Identifying problem areas.
2. Developing learning objectives.
3. Planning instruction.
4. Involving students in the learning process.
5. Determining whether students have learned.
6. Positively reinforcing students.

After analyzing the problem areas and breaking them down into small, teachable parts, you teach the skills and allow time for students to interact and become involved in practice sessions which reinforce the skills taught. Instruction includes introducing new concepts, telling, explaining, demonstrating and reinforcing. By becoming involved with these activities, you can pinpoint problem areas and assess progress of the students. By monitoring progress, you make suggestions, redirect efforts and provide opportunities for students to be successful.

Identifying the Problem Area

An important starting point when assisting students with their assignments, is to diagnose their skill deficiency. When students come to you for academic help, don't assume they know what their problems areas are. They want assistance because they are unable to complete homework and classroom assignments, but they do not necessarily know why they can't complete the work.

Students often don't see the immediate need to prepare for assignments. They do not always come to help sessions adequately prepared or knowledgeable about skill deficiencies. It is your responsibility to quickly identify the problem and help them work toward completing their assignments. They may only come for help just before a major exam or after they have failed an assignment or a test. If students are unable to identify their problem areas, examine copies of their work, or review sections in textbooks or worksheets with them. Another technique, although it takes a little more time, is to administer a short pretest. A pretest will identify what the students know and what they don't know. A pretest doesn't have to be long and usually consists of a few multiple-choice questions. Multiple-choice questions are used because of the ease and quickness of scoring. Pretesting should be used only when you are unable to identify the exact skill deficiency. Results of pretesting let you know which skills the students know and which ones students don't know. Once identified, the instruction which follows deals with what they don't know. Although some material will need to be reviewed, do not spend extended periods of time on skills students already know. Special help sessions are usually limited in time, so the more efficient you are in identifying problem areas, the more time you have for instruction.

When students are having difficulty with subject matter, you may assume either that they are not trying or that they are unable to learn the specified skills. Usually students who need help also need individual diagnosis and special attention from you. It is your job to attempt to pinpoint problem areas and tailor your teaching strategies to meet their individual needs.

Developing Learning Objectives

When problem areas have been identified, learning objectives need to be developed. These objectives will convey to the students what is expected of them. Learning objectives give students precise and concrete information about what is going to happen and what they are going to learn.

Preparing objectives for students coming to you for help should focus on concepts and skills needed to complete their assignments. Classroom instruction often does not sufficiently prepare the students for completing assignments. Therefore, when students come to you for help, you should identify ways to make the out-of-class instruction more effective and meaningful. An attempt should be made to individualize the objectives and to design instruction to meet the needs of the students asking for assistance. The primary aim of learning objectives is to promote learning to the fullest possible extent. Objectives will assist you to be exact, complete and detailed in planning what you are going to teach.

Once a need or a problem area has been identified, it must be broken down into small parts and described in learning objectives. Objectives specify what students are expected to learn. They serve to describe what the students will be able to do at the end of the help session. Each objective should be directly linked to skills you wish to teach and the expected performance of the students. If students know what is expected of them, and if they are motivated to do it, they probably will accomplish the objectives. Without clear objectives, you have no guideline by which to plan their instruction.

Objectives should be manageable and should clearly define what the students will learn and how to determine if they learned it. When preparing for help sessions, state only objectives which are necessary to learn the skills. It is confusing to students to have several concepts presented at once. Small steps must be taken to avoid the common mistake of attempting to teach too much in too short a time. Objectives should be limited to one important concept and presented in such a way that it will be learned properly. Students will learn much better if you don't cram too much information which they don't understand into a limited period of time.

Clearly defined, manageable objectives should be stated as follows:
Find the sum of these addition problems for homework.

Be able to identify the capital cities on a test by Wednesday.

List and describe in writing five factors responsible for terrorism.

Write five sentences using your vocabulary words before class is dismissed.

Objectives state behaviors and describe specifically what the learning experience will be and what the outcome will be. Simply, objectives assist you in putting a situation into words and making the best possible plan. Decide which action has the best possible chance of reaching the goal and proceed with instruction. If you are able to specify objectives in initial planning, you are more likely to be able to evaluate learning outcomes.

When designing instruction for students, you might take note of the following procedures:

Identify objectives for each problem area.

Develop attainable, sequenced steps to obtain objectives.

Plan instruction toward the terminal behaviors.

Focus instruction on individual learners.

Assess progress.

Planning Instruction

Instruction is designed to help students reach the objectives and it begins with a clear statement of what you are going to teach. Once you have developed learning objectives and have decided what content is to be taught and how it is to be taught, instruction is ready to begin.

Planning

When the focus of the lesson is clear, it is time to begin planning for the lesson presentation. Finding out what the students know about the topic is the primary step. If they know nothing about the subject matter, begin at the beginning. If they have some knowledge about the subject matter, find out what they know and what they don't know and begin with the parts they don't know. Provide a smooth transition from what students already know to the new material. It is a common mistake to teach something that is either too difficult or too easy. If you are familiar with the subject matter and the developmental levels of the students, you are likely to plan instruction at the appropriate levels for the individuals within the group.

The first step in lesson preparation is selecting the topic of the lesson. Planning the content requires you to outline step-by-step procedures for instruction. Begin the lesson with simple, concrete facts and move to more difficult, abstract concepts. Organize the content area by defining new terms and sequencing the material into logical steps. A sequence is necessary because parts of the content must be mastered before the students move on to more complex learning. You can make learning skills easier if you get a commitment from the students. Because they are asking for assistance, they are usually ready to commit to learning the material.

Supplemental Material

Students vary substantially in their developmental levels. No teacher can assume that all students in a given grade are able to learn the same content in the same way. It is necessary for you to adapt instructional strategies to the appropriate developmental levels of the learners. As you determine the developmental levels, you will be able to adjust the subject matter in such a way as to provide for all students opportunities for success.

Spending a few minutes reinforcing students prior to teaching them is usually worthwhile. Since many students will be embarrassed because they do not understand the work, work with them on an individual basis and get to know where their difficulties lie. These students may feel more comfortable on a one-to-one basis and be able to participate in a more informal setting when only you are present. Although individual attention is the best way to help students, a small group containing three to five members is appropriate when similar problem areas are identified. In larger groups, not every student will have an opportunity to participate and practice the skills to be learned.

Using supplemental material helps accommodate the individual differences of the learners. Supplemental material also adds richness to the curriculum and guards against boredom. Throughout the school year, students use the same workbooks and textbooks day after day. Supplemental resources reinforce the texts and provide additional practice exercises. Resource material also broadens the scope of the lesson and, when used sensitively, attracts and holds attention.

Select supplemental material and activities that are appropriate to reinforce the identified skills in a logical sequence to the learners. It is essential that you be thoroughly acquainted with the subject matter you are going to teach and that you use the supplemental material to challenge and reinforce what you are trying to teach. Each point in the lesson should relate directly to the stated objectives for students. Materials and resources used to support the lesson content should be selected carefully, keeping in mind the instructional intent. Resource materials, such as books, often provide reinforcement with more concrete experiences within the content area. Textbooks are the most commonly used resources. Encourage the students to use them to support instructional setting. The students who read and review the texts will probably remember the concept longer than the students who don't. Instructional games are interactive and provide opportunities for student participation. Learners analyze problems, make decisions and experience the consequences of their actions. Games enhance learning by involving the students in enjoyable, concrete experiences.

The most regularly used supplemental materials are:

Pencils and Paper	Books	Reference Material
Chalkboards	Tapes	Worksheets
Overhead Projectors	Films	Instructional Games

The selection of appropriate supplemental material is an important task. Select material that is most relevant to the instructional problem.

Instruction

Instruction focuses on individual learners and implements teaching strategies designed to accommodate individual competencies. The content should be well organized and sequenced, and presented in a concrete manner. Students who are having difficulty learning material usually have short attention spans; therefore, you need to adjust instruction to the learners' ability to stay on task. If students are given too much work, it becomes overwhelming and they may not attempt it.

Lecturing to students who are having academic problems does not allow for maximum involvement by the learners. Students who are displaying academic difficulties usually are overwhelmed by the presentation of large amounts of material in short periods of time. Thus, the lecture approach is not the best teaching strategy for meeting individual needs. Students who are experiencing difficulty need active involvement with the content and interaction and feedback from the teacher. Students who have trouble learning abstract concepts might function better when the material is presented in the form of a demonstration. A brief demonstration where students are allowed to actively participate stimulates them and allows them to become involved in the learning process. Small amounts of material can be presented in such a way as to sustain interest in the subject matter. You may have to repeat the demonstration or allow the students to participate in the demonstration. Giving students time to practice the processes enables them to better understand the concepts. Personal comments and the use of examples help maintain the interest of the students. Good examples are clearly stated and relate directly to the subject matter. Descriptive explanations should use a variety of words with which the students are familiar and to which they can relate. Make good use of visual aids and support material and do not explain too much material at one time.

Another technique for involving students in learning activities is to engage them in small group discussion. You may wish to take time for students to discuss a topic and exchange ideas with each other. Your role is to redirect comments to members of the group, rather than to answer the students' questions. Discussion allows students to ask and answer questions and jot down information during the lesson. You might verbally summarize the main points and suggest that they write them down, helping them to focus on the main ideas of the lesson. Teacher- student discussions also help students understand the problem areas and allow them to expand upon the subject matter and to clarify main points. Discussion provides immediate practice sessions and opportunities for feedback.

In order for students to learn, appropriate practice of skills must be allowed. Students must be convinced of the value of practice sessions. They must realize that the more experience they have using skills, the more likely they are to learn them. Most skill learning requires repetition and practice before the skill is learned. The amount of practice varies with each learner. Practice time in the class is often too short for many students. To learn a skill, students must participate in the instructional process. Allow sufficient time for students to practice the skills. A combination of small group practice sessions probably works best when assisting students who need additional help. This method requires that you prepare and present the material to individuals or small groups, and develop stimulating extension work for skill reinforcement.

Pace learning experiences in such a way as to ensure that the learners will experience some amount of success. A good way to bring the lesson to a close is to summarize the main points in the lesson. Cue the learners to the fact that they have reviewed important skills and will be provided with opportunities to practice and reinforce new concepts. If you move too quickly, the students may be turned off by the volume of material and make no attempt to learn it.

To have an effective lesson, use simple and explicit language and keep interest high by using support materials to reinforce skills. Employ sufficient use of examples to make the content more practical. Provide opportunities for questions and organize yourself in such a way as to provide opportunities for evaluation and feedback. A good lesson is one in which a clear concept has been identified and taught successfully within a relatively short period of time.

Effective Teaching Strategies

1. Clarify topic area.
2. Define unfamiliar terms.
3. Use clear and explicit language.
4. Organize lesson in a logical sequence.
5. Involve all students in the lesson.
6. Use appropriate examples.
7. Provide for practice sessions.
8. Use supplemental material.
9. Ask questions.
10. Summarize concepts.

Alternative instructional strategies will be required if students do not learn the material readily. Alternative lessons use diverse instructional materials and require students to engage in different instructional activities. If the skill was taught initially in a large group, the alternative method would be the small group or individual method. Although you should attempt to vary instructional methods, probably no single instructional plan will be perfectly tailored for all students. Each plan has some advantages and some disadvantages. You have to decide what skills students will need to practice and provide opportunities for all students to practice the appropriate amount of time.

Involving Students in the Learning Process

Effective instruction requires students to become actively involved in the learning process. For student participation to be successful, students must be comfortable with you, the teacher, and with small groups of students. You can capitalize on students' natural insights and make them partners in learning rather than merely recipients of teaching. Participation in the learning process requires learners to respond to questions and join in discussions. Students who have skill difficulty may be inhibited and embarrassed about doing classwork since some students criticize and demoralize each other. Before requiring maximum involvement, make sure the students are comfortable in the instructional setting and familiar with the subject matter. You have an important role in directing all students' attention to what they are to be involved in. If you assume that students are focusing in on certain instructional tasks, when in fact they are not, the result will be continuation of skill deficiency.

Small group discussions give the students opportunities to learn subject matter from each other, as well as from you. Cooperative behavior is influenced by you and modeled by the students. The tone of the help session should be structured in such a way that it fosters a non-competitive climate. A non- competitive climate stresses students' productivity and allows them chances for obtaining academic gains. Students working on similar problem areas can be separated into small groups. Most students are willing to work with each other in small groups. Higher performing students often help the lower performing students when teachers encourage this behavior. An atmosphere that encourages students to involve themselves provides a place where you and the students support and help each other.

When students are in small groups, they should be allowed to interact with each other. Verbalizing a concept helps students to remember it. In discussions, students have opportunities to express opinions and clarify their own point of view. Getting learners personally involved is not a simple task. The more advanced students tend to ignore slower members of the group and proceed to dominate the discussion. The students who are having difficulty allow others to dominate because, all too frequently, they are unable to join the discussion. Students need to be encouraged to contribute to the learning process. When you ask simple questions and express support and reinforcement, even the less able learners are likely to join in.

Strategies for Involving Students

1. Call on all students.
2. Ask questions.
3. Require written responses.
4. Provide for small group instruction.

Questioning Strategies

One of the most frequently used techniques in teaching is that of questioning. Although there are many variations in types and rates of questions, an experienced teacher may ask up to 100 questions an hour. Questions request information and are intended to evoke verbal responses and discussions designed to lead students to conclusions. When teachers ask questions, they give students opportunities to use their minds to form concepts. Questioning techniques occupy a central role in the instructional process. About 80 percent of classroom talk is devoted to asking, answering, or reacting to questions. (Barker,1986) There are many reasons for asking questions. Teachers use questions for the following reasons:

1. Actively involve students in the lesson.
2. Focus attention on main ideas.
3. Check for student understanding.
4. Monitor student progress.
5. Diagnose academic difficulties.
6. Summarize and review material.

You, as a teacher, usually believe that the students know most of the answers to the questions and that they will attempt to give accurate responses. Once the response is made, you can assume that the students have become active participants in the lesson. Teacher questions are used to involve the learners. Research suggests that the most common type of questions used are on the lower cognitive levels, specifically memorization and recall. About 60 percent of the questions asked require students only to recall facts or remember information. Higher level questions require students to use existing information to create new information. If students are to be taught at a variety of cognitive levels, a variety of questioning strategies must be used. Teachers who use higher level questioning strategies tend to receive higher level responses from their students. Lower level cognitive questions include data recall, simple deductions, descriptions and interpretations. Examples of lower level questions are:

What is the capital of Florida?

What happens to gas when it is heated?

What is the sum of five plus eight?

What happens when you throw a nail into water?

Higher level questions include hypothesizing, inferring, problem solving, and evaluating. For higher level questions, you could plan questions such as:

What do you think would happen if we put an ice-cube in the sunlight?

How does a cocoon change into a butterfly?

What happens to air when it is heated?

If you were the mayor of this city, what would you do about transportation?

How do you think the country would be different if we had three political parties?

Generally speaking, you should use a variety of cognitive level questions. Good questions don't just happen. They are planned as carefully as the instructional content. All questions should be relevant and reasonable and phrased in a manner which will keep students interested and on their toes. Questions should be stated in a logical sequence and asked throughout the lesson. It might be necessary to repeat or paraphrase questions to reinforce main points. Using commonly understood words increases your questioning effectiveness. Words should be specific and well defined. Superficial and trick questions should be avoided. It is important to adjust questions to the language of the students. Seek to use varied words and combinations of words. Words used over and over tend to become dull and lose their effectiveness. The use of a variety of words adds color and dimension to the questions. Remember to ask questions as often as possible to keep students interested in the lesson. Students should have a reasonable chance of answering the questions. Questions should be clear and within the limits of the students' knowledge. When asking questions, look the students in the eyes and maintain personal contact with them. Once you ask the questions, say nothing and allow a period of time to elapse. The amount of time between the teacher's questions and the students' response is called "wait time." If you, as a teacher, increase wait-time, the length of student responses increases, and a positive climate is set which produces higher cognitive responses. With longer wait-time, students give more organized, well thought out responses and are prone to exhibit more confidence and self-esteem.

Asking questions of students who are unfamiliar with the material could result in incorrect responses and negative reactions to you as teacher. For students who do not understand the material, it would be a good idea to emphasize main ideas before asking the question. One effective way to emphasize main points is to talk at length about the specific point. Repeating important points throughout the lesson and prior to specific questions will cue the students. Since people tend to remember the latest message, summarizing main points throughout the lesson is effective. If the learners still don't answer correctly, the teacher can respond positively in the following ways:

That is a tough question. Bob, let me help you.

Let's check the textbook for a more specific answer.

Good start Mary. Who can help complete the answer?

The use of various questioning techniques usually ensures successful instruction. Merely throwing out a questions rarely achieves the desired results. If you are interested in academic progress, you must develop excellent questioning strategies. Give opportunities to all students to answer questions and accept their responses.

Determining Whether Students Have Learned

The success of assisting students in the learning process depends not only on successful instruction, but on the ability to assess students. Students need to obtain information regarding how well they are performing. Teachers are continuously involved in strategies designed to monitor progress and provide quality feedback to the learners.

Assessment monitors the progress of the students on a continuous basis. It is the primary way strengths are identified and weaknesses can be rectified. It is the basis on which decisions are made. Teachers attempt to identify the information they have at hand and make decisions concerning appropriate instructional strategies.

Evaluating students' progress can be accomplished in many ways. It might consists of one or more of the following:

- Assessment of students' answers to teacher questions.

- Assessment of written responses.

- Assessment of oral discussions.

- Assessment of quizzes, tests, checklists.

- Observation of students.

Students need to know how well they are doing, and they should be provided with teacher feedback. Feedback is one way for students to obtain knowledge about their progress. Continued success occurs when the students are kept informed concerning their progress. Academically assisting students in small groups or individually allows for immediate feedback. Don't assume that the students have learned just because instruction has taken place. All students benefit from being told they are correct or that they are making progress. Since feedback is essential, it should be specific and factual and should communicate progress. Giving students opportunities to demonstrate that they have learned the skills and are able to apply what they learned to new situations will result in positive transfer to new situations.

If after evaluation the students still have not learned the concept, the following checklist should be examined:

1. Were the objectives too difficult for the learner?
2. Did the students have the prerequisite skills necessary for the proposed instruction?
3. Was the content of the instruction appropriate?
4. Did the instructional activities provide skill reinforcement?
5. Was the student motivated and stimulated throughout the instruction?
6. Was the assessment reliable and valid?
7. Was the student provided with regular teacher feedback?

Academically assisting students successfully requires a check to ensure that learning has taken place. It means when students have not learned, that there is a process designed to develop alternative instructional strategies to provide additional information so that future activities will result in learning.

Positively Reinforcing Students

Most students who are having problems with homework assignments, and school work in general, have been negatively conditioned; it is important that they be taught in such a way that they enjoy learning. You need to make them feel welcome by showing them positive regard and support. Your perception of them, as reflected by your behavior, influences how they view themselves and how well they learn. Remember, many of these students receive very little academic success in the classroom. You may be the only one willing to spend the time it takes to help. Therefore, if you have positive view of students' abilities, you send positive messages to them conveying support, realistic expectations and worthiness. If you believe that certain students cannot learn, you will have little success in teaching them. Conversely, if you believe that all students can learn, you will have great success in teaching them. Unfortunately, positive attitudes toward students who are having academic difficulties seem to be at a minimum in schools today. Students who need help with homework assignments and class work need more practice time to learn, more time to answer questions, and more verbal and nonverbal reinforcers. If you are to be effective in helping these students, you will need to develop positive attitudes for all students.

Encourage students to attack problems and to aspire to more understanding of the subject matter by arranging and sequencing the learning steps in such a way as to make success highly probable. Demonstration of respect and positive regard for students allows them to be what they are, without fear of failure. Although you maintain high expectations and confidence that they can accomplish specific work, you guide the learners toward correct responses, allowing them to be successful. Perhaps the single most important activity that you can do with students is to provide an educational atmosphere of success, rather than failure. Fostering a positive outlook and determining reasonable goals for success demonstrates to the students that they are accepted and respected by you.

When assisting students with assignments, be friendly, listen carefully and be willing to help them without finding fault. Students feel more secure when they are not constantly being faulted and ridiculed. In providing a positive and supportive climate, give regular, individual attention and show a continual interest in them. Reinforce the positive climate by using verbal and behavioral reinforcements. Give extra attention to small groups of students and particularly those who make an effort to complete their work. Many students who are having academic difficulty will not attempt to complete their work or interact with others. Make a point of talking with all students and speak to them individually during work sessions. Asking questions and making comments shows them that you are personally interested in them. Personal attention from you contributes significantly to the students' self esteem and the feeling that you are available to help them.

Verbal reinforcers show support and encouragement to the learners. They increase student attention and work output. Strive to provide on-going, enthusiastic reinforcement to all students on a regular basis. Enthusiastic teachers have students who tend to respond positively to the subject matter presented and their enthusiasm in conveyed through genuine interest in the subject matter. When you express enthusiasm, you promote greater academic gain in your students. It is vital that you reserve time for one-to-one contact with all students. During your help sessions, make personal comments or verbally reinforce the students. These chats can be held while you are helping the students or while you are waiting for the bell or before you are ready to begin instruction. The habit of responding to all students is important in maintaining a positive climate.

If students are working and being productive, notice the gains and provide positive feedback to them:

- That's a good answer. Let's summarize this section.

- You've completed a lot of work today. You learned how to add two digit numbers.

- Good start. Do you need help with the next one?

- Those are great answers, Courtney. Does anyone remember two more reasons?

- Those are not all right. Let me help you correct them.

Clear, direct comments are far more appropriate than vague ones. Students are more likely to respond to comments which are personal and based on honest observations of performance. Compliments spoken with no justification tune students out and result in negative feelings. Students are quick to spot conflicts between what you say and how you behave. Letting students know you are there to help them and will respond to them honestly sets a comfortable learning tone.

When you react in a positive, relaxed way, and reinforce learners through praise and nonverbal behavior, students respond with good attitudes and motivation to learn. When you treat students as worthwhile people, regardless of success or failure, barriers are removed. Students will be more likely to attempt the homework problems when this climate prevails. When students are not punished for making too many errors and when they are very interested in the material, the outcomes will be positive. These methods of assistance usually ensure a successful climate and should be used with students who have experienced limited success in the past.

Reducing Anxiety in Students

As school work becomes more difficult, there is frequently a build-up in tension in students. Many students feel uncomfortable in an academic setting because of previous unsuccessful school experiences. It is common knowledge that when students are having skill difficulty, they tend to avoid school work. It is important to implement strong motivational procedures into basic instruction with students who are behind. As we view these students, we will not see all smiles and enthusiasm. Students who have met with successive failure frequently develop negative emotional attitudes. These students repel teacher overtures and often sulk throughout the lesson. Disruptive behavior, such as giggles and excessive talking, are frequently signs that the subject matter has become too threatening for the students. Disruptive behavior usually interrupts the learning experience and needs to be dealt with positively. Respond to the disruptive behavior by maintaining focus on the task at hand and proceeding through the problem area in an organized and sequenced manner.

When students don't do well or fail, they blame their grades on factors such as teachers, home, outside activities, or difficulty of assignments. They formulate excuses as to why they didn't score well or pass the exams. Most students want to project a positive image, which includes, among other things, academic competence; so they are motivated to gain acceptance by operating successfully. Once these students succeed, their expectations increase and they are likely to continue improving. Likewise, if they are not helped academically, the students with lower scores will display decreased academic motivation and feel more negative about school work. The attitude and feelings of the students are important aspects of the effectiveness of the learning atmosphere. Almost all teachers have had experiences in which there appears to be friction or hostility in the group.

There are many reasons for students not completing work:

1. Poor reading ability.
2. Class work too difficult.
3. Instructional pace too fast.
4. Lack of time to complete work.
5. Inability to understand and follow directions.
6. Not enough individual attention and assistance.
7. Short attention span.
8. Absence of resource materials.
9. Lack of interest.
10. Intimidation of slower students by brighter students
11. Frustration at not learning subject matter.
12. Poor writing ability.
13. Lack of teacher feedback.
14. Behavior problems.

You must treat all students with dignity and respect and remain sensitive to their needs. Helping them understand why you want to assist them is a beginning. Informing them of your goals and moving them toward the attainment of the goals decreases tension. Most students will cooperate with you, unless what you are asking them to do is too difficult. Seating students around a table or in a half circle is an easy way to maintain close contact with them. When the seating arrangement is intimate, small groups can assist each other and share view points. Examples of statements to show students you want to help them are:

- I can see you are becoming impatient. Let's work on number seven together.

- I am here to help you understand photosynthesis. Let's start by defining what it means.

- I would like to help you complete your algebra assignment. When did you begin having difficulty?

If you don't establish a positive climate and begin with a positive statement, the students are likely to think you don't want to help them. By making your intent clear and by appearing supportive, the likelihood of negative behavior diminishes. When assisting students academically, it is necessary that you develop a free interchange of information and ideas with the students. Your job is to facilitate this effort by encouraging participation and commitment. If students continue to display hostility and withdrawal, you may have them talk about their concerns and get them back on-task as quickly as possible. Airing student concerns often reduces emotions and tension. Because of high demands on students, many of them feel inadequate and are unable to proceed with school work. Many of these students don't know what they are supposed to do or how they are going to do it. Some will wait to see how much of the assignment they are actually responsible for, before attempting to complete the task. It is important that you clearly assign the task, announce the limitations and due dates, and individually assist students who need help. Troubled students are overwhelmed by academic pressures and need to be encouraged with patience and understanding. Without encouragement, disinterest and lack of motivation to complete work can continue to develop. You can help students see themselves as winners. Students who have problems with work assignments often view themselves negatively. Failures and inadequacies give them lots of ammunition for self-criticism. These negative feelings are reinforced by continued poor grades. Remind them that you are there to assist them in a logical and systematic way. If you maintain an emphatic approach to the problem by becoming involved with the students and by identifying and clarifying the problem, the students are more likely to become involved with solving their own problems because they trust you to help them. Examples of encouraging comments follow:

- It looks as though you are having difficulty finishing your work. Why don't you take a five minute break.

- I'll wait a minute until you're ready.

- Elizabeth, we need your ideas to help us solve the problem.

- Let's review the problem before we begin the assignment.

- You are doing very well in science. From the looks of this, we will need to spend time on math today.

Work with troubled students, helping them solve their own problems. Allowing the students to compromise and bargain often wastes time and is not generally effective. Once the tone is set for completing the work, remain in control and share your enthusiasm, but don't accept less than what is expected. It is important to express concern for students and let them know you are there to help them, without alienating or threatening them.

When instruction is well planned and structured to achieve stated goals, student anxiety and hostility is minimized. If you don't know the subject matter and don't keep the students interested in the task at hand, don't be surprised if students become uninterested or hostile. If there are still students refusing to work and continuing to exhibit troublesome behavior, other techniques may be necessary. After subject matter has become associated with failure, the student will find it difficult to keep his mind on it. When assisting these students, you may have to identify their problem areas for them. Once identified, these areas may be broken down into several smaller parts. A single skill should be presented clearly, without rambling or presenting ideas that are not pertinent to the problem. Further clarification may be necessary, but wandering from the central theme will cause students to become distracted and disinterested. It may be necessary to reinforce the concept with games or puzzles that exert little academic pressure. Usually after a short period of time, the non-threatening activity will interest and involve the students. Once students have gained confidence in their learning ability, more concepts can be taught successfully.

Students who are interested in the subject matter are more likely to spend time on it. Many students do not complete assignments because of lack of interest and, as time goes on, their lack of knowledge increases. Students often lose interest because they fail to see how the subject matter will benefit them. If students lack interest, try to get them involved in an activity that they like. If you identify several students having difficulty with the same problem, ask them to work in pairs. Working with peers can make students feel more comfortable. Suggestions on how to relate previously learned material follow:

- What math operations will we use to find out the batting averages of today's game?

- We spoke about ecology yesterday. How does ecology differ from conservation?

- What are some of reasons we have a two party system? Joe, would you summarize your ideas for us?

Structure the help sessions in such a way as to capitalize on the students' interests and strengths. Focus on helping students to maximize their successes, while maintaining their interest in the subject matter.

Summary

This chapter offered suggestions for helping students learn. Students often fail to learn in classroom situations for many reasons. Some of the reasons include: lack of interest, tension and low achievement. Plans for academically assisting students should include focusing instruction on individual learners. Alternative instructional strategies are usually required when assisting students who are having difficulty with assignments.

Six major components of instruction were discussed: identifying problem areas, developing learning objectives, planning instruction, involving students in the learning process, determining whether students learned, and positively reinforcing students. This chapter described an instructional plan whereby teachers can successfully assist students who need academic help. When students are treated with respect and positive regard, and taught in an appropriate way, they are more likely to attempt difficult academic assignments.

3 A Positive Approach to Learning

The environment students have access to has a great impact on the development of self concept and the learning process. Since many students who come to you need assistance with assignments, you have the responsibility of planning for a positive environment with emphasis on warmth, support, reinforcement and success. Much of your time should be spent on creating and maintaining an atmosphere that is friendly and filled with acceptance and encouragement. A supportive climate has positive effects on learning. It establishes mutual support and respect between students and teachers and fosters positive relationships among students.

Guidelines for Creating a Positive Classroom Climate

Positive classroom climates provide the framework within which you and the students function cooperatively. Good classroom climate helps you establish expectations by assuming all students are worthy and important and able to learn. Warm and supportive classrooms display high expectations for student performance and support the belief that the successful education of learners is important.

The effective teacher identifies the needs of the students and is aware of their attitudes and beliefs. The teacher then carefully plans lessons using a variety of teaching methods which will allow for optimum learning to take place in a comfortable climate. Students relate well to teachers who show friendliness in a non-threatening place. Students need to know they can make mistakes without fear of reprisal from the teacher. They need to know that errors are part of the learning process and that successful experiences will follow. Teacher effectiveness requires that you understand individuals within the classroom. It is essential that the classroom reflects to the students the feeling that help is available to them. This feeling of assurance and support fosters positive attitudes toward learning. Help should be given in a positive fashion without ridicule from you. Arrange your days so that every student experiences success on a regular basis. Each student should experience a positive acknowledgement from you every day. The following guidelines give suggestions for providing a positive classroom climate:

Guidelines for Positive Climate

Do you speak clearly and succinctly?

Do you allow students to ask questions?

Do you show an interest in your students?

31

Is your room warm and cheerful?

Do you speak without yelling and threatening?

Do you encourage students to assume leadership roles?

Are you consistent?

Are you flexible?

Do you help students when they need help?

Do you praise students every day?

Are you fair to students?

Do you help students find acceptable ways to express themselves?

Enhancing Self Esteem in Students

Positive self esteem comes when we feel happy as a result of our needs being satisfied. Our degree of self esteem determines how we perceive the world, how we act, how we learn and how we work. Self esteem may help determine a student's success in school. When a student feels good about himself, he usually exhibits behavior that promotes his self esteem. A student who feels good about his academic success is likely to want to continue the good feelings brought on by the successful experience by continuing to succeed academically. Students with positive self esteem exhibit confidence, independence, pride, responsibility and general enthusiasm about learning. Students with low self esteem will blame others, make excuses, behave defensively, and avoid anxious or stressful situations.

High Self Esteem Students

Students with high self esteem generally like school and get satisfaction from their experiences in school. They usually perform well in school and attempt more difficult projects than students with low self esteem. These students seek praise and approval to try to do things well in order to please significant others. These students are proud of their accomplishments and assume responsibility for their actions. Students with high self esteem have good relationships with others. They seek out people to reinforce their feelings about themselves and they are secure enough to risk developing new relationships and feel good when significant others praise them.

Examples of behaviors displayed by high self esteem students are:

Confidence	—	"I'm sure I completed this assignment correctly."
Independence	—	"I decided what my topic will be for my science project."
Pride	—	"My latest book report is my best effort so far this year."
Responsibility	—	"I will recheck all my assignments."

32

Enthusiasm — "I feel great about my academic accomplishments so far this year."

Low Self Esteem Students

Students with low self esteem do not like school. They have little interest in learning and are unable to pay attention and listen in class, causing them to perform poorly in the academic areas. As these students progress through the grades, they fall further behind in basic skills. These students are easily frustrated and highly anxious about new situations. They have difficulty making friends and socializing, causing them to be isolated from group experiences. Students with low self esteem have negative attitudes not only about themselves, but their environment in general. They reject praise and resist participating in school related activities. They are usually overly aggressive when they feel they are not liked or accepted by a group of peers.

Behaviors exhibited by low self esteem students include:

Blaming Others — "You didn't explain this assignment to me."

Excuses — "I didn't do my homework because I had to go to football practice."

Defensive Behavior — "I gave my assignment to Judy to hand in for me."

Anxious Behavior — "I'm not going to school today. I have an algebra test."

Self Esteem of Parents

The self esteem of parents is often modeled by their children. Parents with high self esteem act in ways that promote positive self esteem in their children. These parents help their children set and achieve goals and maintain realistic expectations for reaching goals. These parents provide an environment that encourages independence and responsibility and they give their children opportunities to participate in decision making and problem solving situations in everyday life.

Parents with low self esteem have difficulty communicating with their children. They do not listen to their children and set unrealistic goals for them. Often they encourage their children to achieve much higher than the children are intellectually able. Thus the children meet with repeated failures, and their parents continue to ridicule and threaten them. Parents with low self esteem have difficulty praising their children and tend not to praise them at all. Rather, they argue with their children and are often overly critical of them.

Parents are significant people in the lives of their children. If parents belittle or reject their children, the children are likely to develop poor self esteem. Other significant people in the lives of these children are teachers, peers and siblings. Significant people are important in students' development of self esteem. How they perceive others feel about them and what they are doing helps determine how they will feel about themselves. When children feel accepted by their parents, they are likely to display warm and accepting feelings towards others. They are able to accept themselves as valuable and worthy people. Accepting parents are warm, supporting, patient and caring with their children. Since parents are in control of many aspects of their children's lives, they have a direct impact on their children's perceptions of themselves. All children should feel they are special by seeing continued evidence of adequacy and self worth. The way parents interact everyday with their children has a great impact on their self esteem.

Enhancing Self Esteem

Treat students as unique individuals

Help students set realistic and attainable goals

Help students make decisions and solve problems

Tell students you feel good about them

Reinforce and praise students

Listen without making judgments

Be a good model

Communicate and share feelings

Find positive ways to resolve conflicts

Give every student attention every day

Touch students

Help students feel included

Teacher Expectations

People usually behave according to expectations. We learn early in life to identify what specific behaviors will elicit positive responses or praise from significant people in our environment. People need clear ideas about what is expected of them. Effective teachers state their expectations to their students in a clear, succinct manner.

When you set high and reasonable goals for students, you are likely to get positive results. The opposite is also true. When low standards are set for students, usually negative results are seen. To be effective, you need to develop a set of expectations concerning how the students will perform. Teachers who do not believe a group of students can perform well academically display a low set of expectations. If you had low expectations, you might be heard to say, "I know these exercises are so difficult that most of you won't attempt them." If you had high expectations, you might state your feelings in a more positive way, such as, "I know these are difficult exercises, but do the best you can."

Some appropriate teacher expectations might include:

- Students will do assignments three nights a week.
- All homework will be graded.
- Students will hand in all assignments on time.
- Students will attend class regularly.
- Students will take a quiz every Thursday in math.

Teacher expectations may need to be modified for specific students who are having difficulties. If a student is encountering academic difficulties, the teacher should have a regular plan for dealing with the difficulty and communicating it to the student. If a student is having difficulty with math, he may be assigned homework five days a week until he catches up. On the other hand, if he is doing well, he may be assigned homework only one day that week. Teachers who have reasonable expectations usually get positive results from their students. Students need to know what is expected of them. They want the adults in their lives to be consistent with their expectations. The following are examples of ways to enhance the self esteem of students:

Establishing Rules

You must use rules to establish parameters of behaviors. Rules are guidelines used to achieve and maintain order and structure. A good rule must define the task students may or may not do. Rules reduce uncertainty and confusion. They are intended to allow for fair treatment of all involved. It is the your responsibility to present, explain, discuss and monitor the set of rules. The rules must be reasonable for all parties and be enforceable. A clear set of expectations of what is acceptable must be established.

Instead of saying to the student, "Stop talking and finish your work," it would be better to say, "You have fifteen minutes to complete your math work." You should state rules precisely:

- Work will begin promptly at 8:45.
- All work must be completed neatly.
- There will be no talking until all work is completed.

It is easier to start with a small number of short, reasonable rules and add to them or modify them if they are not enforceable. Rules must be regularly reviewed and understood by the students and must be stated in a positive way. Displaying rules in a conspicuous place serves as a reminder to the students.

Maintaining Consistency

Teachers often have a difficult time maintaining consistency. Inconsistencies occur when adults react differently toward different students for the same behaviors. Inconsistencies also occur when adults react differently toward the same student for the same behavior, occurring at different times. Often rules are established but not enforced by the person responsible for the maintenance of the rules. When a set of rules becomes unenforceable, the rules should be modified, rather than treated with inconsistency. Students work better in an environment where they know what is expected of them and are clear about the consequences of not adhering to the rules. If a set of procedures is unreasonable or unworkable and difficult to monitor, a climate of uncertainty will develop. Inconsistencies in the use of rules will cause confusion about what is acceptable behavior. Students frequently "test the limits" by not following the rules , often causing the teacher to tolerate high levels of inappropriate behavior. On the other hand, there may be an appropriate set of rules, which the adult fails to follow.

Dealing with Inappropriate Behavior

Inappropriate behaviors that students display include lack of involvement in learning activities, inattention, aggression, violation of rules, fighting and disruptions. Each adult that works with young people needs to define, in his own terms, the behaviors that are appropriate. Once that definition is completed, prompt handling of inappropriate behavior is necessary to avoid the continuation of the behaviors. One effective way to do this is through prevention. You can strive to provide an environment where behavior problems are unlikely to occur. Structuring the environment in such a way, often prevents inappropriate behaviors from beginning. Those of you who devote considerable time to planning and preparing for lessons are less likely to provide opportunities for inappropriate behavior because you are engaging students in well planned lessons and meaningful activities. Involving students in the learning process is instrumental in creating a positive and active learning environment.

Adults who work with young people occasionally have to contend with offensive and inappropriate behavior. A good system must deal quickly and effectively with the problem behavior. All students want "approval." Approval is related to satisfaction and success. Ignoring minor inappropriate behavior should cause it to decrease. In most instances, it is wise to correct inappropriate behavior in the initial stages, before it gets out of hand. Students who are taught appropriate behavior techniques will continue to build on this type of behavior because they find they can receive attention from good behavior.

The first step in dealing with inappropriate behavior is to determine the specific inappropriate behavior. Whenever possible let the students know exactly what is acceptable and what is not. It is wise to ignore minor disruptions and problems. Although sometimes it is difficult to know when to ignore minor inappropriate behavior, behaviors that are of short duration and do not bother other members of the class can be ignored. These behaviors might include writing, whispering, day dreaming, or exhibiting short intervals of off-task behavior. To react to these minor behaviors would consume time and energy that could best be spent on teaching. The next step in dealing with inappropriate behavior is to

teach the student what is acceptable and what is not acceptable. Begin w
is easy to learn and one that will contribute to the student's success.

Ways to Encourage Student Participation

Students often do not attempt to complete academic exercises. Man,
interested in the assignment and resist adult attempts to involve them. The following ideas
will help to get the students to participate in homework activities:

1. Assign high interest work.
2. Keep assignments short.
3. Give students several options for work assignments.
4. Personalize the work assignments.
5. Allow students to ask questions to clarify assignments.
6. Review skills needed to successfully complete assignments.
7. Give time in class to begin assignments.
8. Provide academic assistance to those students needing it.
9. Assign "group" projects.
10. Allow students to create their own assignments.

There are several ways to encourage students to stay "on task":

- Redirection to task at hand

- Reminder of rules

- Use of proximity

- Use of eye contact

- Offer of academic assistance

- Provision of incentives for work completion

- Allowance of no excuses

Nonverbal Communication

Nonverbal communication is a critical aspect of interpersonal communication in the
classroom. Students feel more positive affect for teachers who nonverbally communicate
warmth and support. Your touch is a good way to communicate trust. Various studies have
found teacher warmth and friendliness to be important predictors of positive student
response toward teachers, subject matter and school in general. Many of the cues students
use to make judgments about you are obtained by observing your nonverbal behavior. You
regularly send messages to students to reinforce their learning. Smiles, eye contact or
nodding heads help students know if what they are doing is correct. Positive nonverbal
behaviors that can be observed include:

smile	silence	proximity
frown	eye contact	foot movement
hand movement	head movement	facial expression
gesture	posture	appearance

Verbal Communication

Another important way to promote a supportive climate is to create a positive communicative flow between teachers and students. Verbal reinforcement provides rewards for behavior we approve of in others. The verbal messages that you use have an important effect on students. Positive messages are used to encourage, guide and support behavior that is appropriate. You are a constant source of communicative messages in the classroom and these messages can have either a positive or negative impact on student learning. A supportive teacher will teach students to behave in appropriate ways and will allow them to positively communicate with fellow students.

Teacher Praise

Praise usually promotes learning. Teacher praise, when used appropriately, is very effective with students. It is wise to praise students for correct performance and behavior. All people appreciate hearing good things about themselves and most students respond positively to praise in all grade levels. Some students need more praise than others and wise teachers are able to identify those students quickly. Although praise works well with most students, some do not know how to accept praise and seem to ignore people who praise them. These students are often secondary level students who will respond more positively if the praise is given privately and in a calm, professional fashion. If the student continues to exhibit inappropriate behavior when praised, you might consider the use of another type of reward.

Generally praise and attention should be given to behaviors which facilitate learning. Examples of times to praise include:

- When the student is exhibiting good study habits.

- When the student is staying "on task."

- When the student is displaying appropriate behavior.

Praise should be used on a regular basis by you as well as parents. It should be offered in a natural and comfortable way. Highlighting behavior, even when it is positive, sometimes embarrasses the student, causing a negative reaction to praise. Effective teachers know when and how to praise effectively. Some examples of effective praise follow:

- Praise for specific academic performance.

- Praise for work completion.

- Praise for prior academic performance.

- Praise for difficult tasks.

- Praise for future academic performance.

- Praise for special projects.

Words of Approval

great	neat	o.k.
yes	nice	good thinking
good	outstanding	super job
super	fabulous	well done
fascinating	terrific	nice work
clever	perfect	great job
correct	right	good performance
creative	wonderful	that's interesting
superior	imaginative	nice thoughts
thorough	thoughtful	you're doing fine
wow	excellent	you've got it
magnificent	fantastic	good work

Words of Encouragement

that's better	you are doing better
you are improving	good progress
I can tell you are trying	satisfactory work
do your best work	good thinking
keep up the good work	your project was creative

Building a Reward System

When you want a student to learn a new behavior, reward the specific behavior every time it occurs. Rewards are used to strengthen acceptable behavior immediately after the behavior occurs. If the student begins to exhibit the appropriate behavior and feels positive about the results of it, he usually repeats the behavior. For example, when the student who habitually hands in incomplete homework assignments begins to hand in completed homework exercises, reward him every time he does so. The student must be rewarded immediately and regularly until his new behavior becomes "regular" behavior. At that point, it is no longer necessary to give rewards 100 percent of the time. After that period, the rewards should be given intermittently to reinforce and maintain the new behavior. If a student who never completes homework assignments, begins completing 50 percent of them, rewards can be given for partial completion. It is important to remember that the goal should be 100 percent completion, and the student should be rewarded for improvement until he completes all the assignments. Again, once the student regularly completes the homework assignments, he should be rewarded occasionally to reinforce and maintain the behavior. You might reward students for the following improvements:

- Taking books and supplies home
- Completing part of homework assignments
- Making an attempt to complete assignments
- Completing all homework assignments
- Maintaining appropriate study environment
- Improving homework grades
- Finding academic assistance when necessary

Too many teachers reward undesirable behavior by paying too much attention to it. A teacher may raise her voice or threaten students, causing an unpleasant environment. Instead, pay attention to disorderly students only when they act appropriately. If students continue to act inappropriately, it is often difficult to reward them. You sometimes have to teach students new or appropriate behaviors and reward them when they display those desirable behaviors. It is difficult to reward students who are not nice. You often don't trust these students to continue with the positive behavior and tend to ignore even the positive behavior. Be sure that appropriate behavior has an immediate pay-off for the student. Exhibiting inappropriate behavior often gets the students what they want, attention from you, even though that attention is negative attention.

Behaviors that are unrewarded will eventually extinguish themselves. Behaviors that are partially reinforced are the most difficult to extinguish. If a problem behavior occurs frequently, one can be certain that it has been positively reinforced. If students can get attention by not completing assignments, they probably won't complete them. The following list shows ways that you can reinforce behavior that is not appropriate:

- Do not grade homework when not handed in on time.
- Only grade "specified" assignments.
- Allow students "extra" time in class to complete homework.
- Threaten to inform parents about incomplete homework assignments.

Never reinforce negative behavior by providing an environment in which it can occur. Do not pay attention to the behavior by arguing with students, doing the activity for them, or giving in to them. You can implement a reward system for reinforcement of positive behavior. The following lists give examples of positive school rewards:

School Rewards

touch
proximity
stickers
stamps
toys
trinkets
ribbons
certificates
cards
buttons
money

grades
credit
pictures
materials
games
supplies
posters
tapes
tickets
points
books

Social Rewards

letters to parents
names on board
special class privileges
teacher as partner
special passes
free time
class leader
computer time
written reinforcement
teacher/student lunch

care of class pets
supervise class activities
perform as teacher assistant
homework "break"
specified parking space
citizenship award
first choice for team mates
access to classroom
access to music

Home Rewards

parental praise
designating special time with parents
hugging
smiling
extending telephone time
extending curfew time
taking trips with parents

using "adult tools"
recognition by family and friends touching
taking student to lunch or dinner
giving extra money
preparing a favorite dinner
giving free time from chores
buying a special toy

Reluctant Learner

Students who have not had successful academic experiences usually are non-motivated, reluctant learners. Many students in our schools today are underachievers. Many of these students are mentally able to do well in school, but they don't achieve up to their potential. Such underachievement is prevalent in all schools and at all levels of intelligence. Since the drive to learn underlies all educational achievement, schools can help students develop their potentials.

Studies have shown that generally students with low self esteem were less cooperative, uninterested and low achievers. These students often had negative self esteem and did not like school. They had a high rate of absenteeism and were often tardy for classes. They usually did not complete homework, had poor study habits, and were not interested in obtaining high grades. Students tended to participate in activities in which they were successful and avoided activities in which they were likely to fail. Frequent failures at home and at school caused these students to have low expectations, and they reacted by becoming easily discouraged and prone to giving up. They usually had short attention spans and were less willing to complete assignments. Often these students were placed in groups or classes where competition and extra work were expected. Many of the students were unable to keep up with the pace and became discouraged and lost confidence in their ability to do the work. In situations like these, it is crucial to move the students to different groups or classes in order to eliminate the academic pressures and restore successful experiences and self esteem.

Another common characteristic found in reluctant learners was evidence of low energy levels. These students were considered "lazy" by both teachers and parents. When they did not have many successful experiences they quickly lost interest in school and focused their physical energy elsewhere. Reluctant learners often displayed signs of boredom for any school related topic and provided a difficult situation for teachers.

Effective teachers are enthusiastic teachers. When reluctant students spent time with enthusiastic teachers, they appeared to regain interest in academic areas. If you display enthusiasm in class, it will energize students by conveying to them a real interest in the subject matter and zeal for learning in general. Use voice tones, body language, eye contact, proximity and gestures to teach subject matter, thus motivating students. A variety of teaching styles should be implemented and various teaching materials used to help maintain an exciting learning environment for all students.

Sensitivity to students' needs and feelings is important in breaking the cycle of the reluctant learner. It is evident that different students respond in different ways to the same classroom situation. Reluctant learners are usually not cooperative and do not take criticism well. These students often become hostile and belligerent. These negative feelings are evident in the student's social life as well as in his home life. You can help students capitalize on their strengths by creating situations in which they can succeed, thus breaking the underachievement cycle. Communicate to underachievers positively, thereby helping them to modify their self concepts.

These characteristics of reluctant learners suggest that teachers must give special consideration to understanding students and establishing procedures and rules that will build their self esteem.

Motivated Learners

Responsible, independent and motivated students learn more and learn faster than low achieving, reluctant learners. Motivated learners allow teachers to spend less time in classroom management and discipline and more time in teaching. These students are curious about the "how" and the "why" of things and need to be challenged by finding answers for questions, solving problems and learning in a setting where creative discovery is valued. Students' interests are important elements for learning, and skillful teachers relate student interests to subject matter. Students' interest in marine biology may lead them to doing a book report exploring recent marine findings and the times and places in which they happened.

One aspect of motivation over which you have considerable control is the interest and challenge of the immediate situation. The environment contains resources that are attractive or unattractive. School activities may not be attractive if they appear either too difficult or too easy. Even motivated learners shun activities if they are too long and mechanical. Motivated students usually have continuous academic success and they realize increased levels of aspirations. If students continuously "fail," they accept failure and their levels of aspirations decline over the years. The longer the failure cycle continues, the more difficult it is to overcome.

Generally students will be motivated to achieve academically if they know what is expected from them, if they know that their work will be evaluated and valued, if they expect to be successful, if they have previously been successful and if they think the assignment will be worthwhile.

Summary

A positive classroom climate is based on students understanding what is expected of them. Continuously strive for an emotional climate that is warm, supportive and friendly, rather than one that is cold, unpleasant and uncomfortable. If students experience the spirit of support and warmth, they will seek to do what it takes to maintain a sense of well-being. If, on the other hand, students experience hostility and anger, they will be less likely to positively attend to appropriate learning tasks. Your intent is to create a classroom climate that helps students feel secure and comfortable, therefore enhancing their self esteem. You must decide on class rules and a system where all students receive attention, praise and success. Being able to communicate expectations and rules is critical for classroom success. You need to be actively involved in maintaining high self esteem in students by increasing student participation in learning activities and by reducing boredom, confusion, and failure.

4

Effective Communication Strategies

Communication is more than just the sending and receiving of messages. Successful communication depends on the receiver's correct interpretation of the message. Thus communication involves the development of human relationships and mutual understanding between people. Communication is the flow of information from one person to another. It is a complex, continuous process where we share experiences through words, expressions, body movement and touch. Human communication connects people by stimulating their minds through verbal and nonverbal messages. When we talk to people, we share descriptions, explanations, events, ideas, feelings and opinions.

In order for communication to be effective, the participants must be able to process information and assign meaning to the messages. Communication requires an active response by the participant to the verbal and non verbal messages given off, thus creating the state of being understood. When we understand, we see the world as the other person sees it and accurately predict meanings.

There are many times when we don't communicate with others as well as we would like. Different needs, experiences, perceptions and backgrounds can cause problems in communication exchange. Achieving a good communication flow requires knowledge of the participants and the mutual activity of giving and receiving messages through correct interpretation and understanding. Students learn from non-verbal message as well as verbal messages. If good communication is to occur, teachers must take the initiative not only by giving the information, but by participating in the response. When teachers take pains to communicate with their students, the students become more responsive to the teacher and the academic setting in general.

Teacher Communication

The ability to communicate is an essential skill of teaching. Teachers are the constant source of communicative messages. Effective communication involves the ability to both give and receive messages. You must understand the students' problems before you can begin to help them. The instructional format should be well organized, concise and clear, maintaining student interest by actively involving students in the solving of problems. A warm, informal setting gives more assurance that each student will be motivated to work up to his individual level of competence. A climate develops as people spend time together. Feelings of trust, freedom of expression and group loyalty are ingredients of a positive classroom climate. Many students who come to you for assistance have not listened or communicated well with their classroom teachers. Students are more likely to stay on task when you provide a reinforcing environment and opportunities for students to interact.

The best way for you to feel confident is to know subject matter and to understand what you are going to say. Students often become confused by rambling teachers who fail to get to the point. You decide what important facts to talk about and then narrow them down and manage them in the allotted time. Once you decide on your primary focus, you should introduce high interest material. Remember, it is difficult to maintain interest if the presentation is boring. When students are stimulated by the subject matter and provided with interesting support material, they will pay more attention and actively listen to what you are teaching. You attract students when you appeal to their desire to know new things. Presenting new material in an interesting and creative way helps students understand facts about the subject. Personal experiences and examples are often told to maintain student interest. The best stories are short and get to the point quickly. Using too many words will diminish the effect of the story and lose audience interest. You should search for vivid and descriptive words that picture the information you are trying to get across. If students are required to read a chapter or report, it is your responsibility to assure that all students have copies of the text or printed material.

When discussion occurs, you should maintain as much eye contact as possible. One way to ensure good eye contact is to seat students in a half circle. When students are positioned in a half circle, it is easy to move around to face the students. Another way to stimulate student interest is to use poster presentation for summarization. The print of the words should be large enough for all to see and the poster should be read to the students because some may not be able to read it without help. Another way to emphasize important points is to ask students to refer to a specific page and summarize the material for them. If this is done in an enthusiastic manner, the students will more likely stay on task and ask questions to assist them in understanding the material. If the entire section is read to them, you will lose credibility and if you stumble or appear unsure, you will lose your authority. Students react not only to what you say, but to how you say it. They not only listen to you, but they also look at you. Therefore, when you teach a lesson to the class, position yourself so all can see you, present a pleasant appearance, be enthusiastic, clear, simple and short.

Effective teacher communication consists of not only imparting and conveying information, but knowing how to say it. Good communication is instrumental in determining the type and amount of participation and interaction.

Effective Communication Strategies for Teachers

- Make sure all students understand rules and schedules.

- Make enthusiastic opening comments.

- Set the climate for positive instruction.

- Give clear, precise directions.

- Call on all students.

- Maintain eye contact

- Ask and answer questions.

- Allow students to exchange ideas.

- Paraphrase student responses.

- Provide immediate feedback.

- Schedule time for group discussion.

- Explain grading procedures thoroughly.

- Be responsive to students.

Improving Listening Skills

We spend more time each day listening than we spend on any other form of communications. Most people spend approximately 70 percent of their waking hours in some form of communication and about 45 percent of that time listening to others. It has been said that 85 percent of all that we know is gained from listening. We listen at an average rate of 200 words per minute, although our comprehension rate is about 400 words per minute. This means we have plenty of time to hear the words and still be distracted by thinking of other things at the same time. Effective listening requires energy, involvement and patience. Trying to make sense of a multitude of facts and issues is extremely difficult. Many students in our schools are ill equipped to manipulate and use the information they receive, or to appreciate it.

Students must be physically able to hear the sounds of language, to distinguish among language sounds and to assign meaning to them. Once they have completed this, they must sort out significant information from non significant information and be able to comprehend the content of the message. The listener then must analyze and draw comparisons and relationships and make generalizations regarding the information. Listening is a skill that requires students to participate in both processing and responding behaviors. Responding behaviors include questioning, commenting on subject matter or performing an activity. Listening is more than just receiving sounds, processing those sounds and making sense of the information received.

Students can easily acquire poor listening habits if classroom discussions and presentations discourage active responses. Many students have never been required to become active listeners. You often set a framework for poor listening skills to develop. Practices such as oral reading, lengthy reports and long lectures usually bore students to distraction. There are many other reasons why students don't listen well. Lack of interest in subject matter may affect students' attitudes and get in the way of listening. Teacher mannerisms also may distract the student from listening. Behavior such as rapid blinking, staring, facial tics, or excessive hand movements often cause students to lose interest. Physical distractions such as hot rooms, noisy corridors, flickering lights are all roadblocks to listening. You can help students become better listeners by giving them practice in purposeful, active and critical listening. Teach such skills as listening for main ideas, following directions, recognizing speaker's intent and generalizing content of message.

Increasing Understanding

One of the most important communication variables in the classroom is the ability to select appropriate information from verbal and nonverbal messages and make sense of it. We make sense of messages by accurately decoding and encoding. When we listen, we do not always attend to all the words that are spoken. Instead, we tend to select words and parts of sentences. We then organize these auditory stimuli into sensible patterns and determine a response. What appears to be informative and appropriate to you may not always be received positively by the students; thus, poor listening skills develop. Students with poor listening skills often miss crucial aspects of the content being communicated. Communication can occur only if the listener actively listens and understands the speaker and vice-versa. Some students are poor listeners because they are unwilling to listen. They may have negative attitudes toward learning and tend to disapprove of the instructional situation. These students often become wrapped up in themselves and in their peer involvements and just don't pay attention to what you are saying.

You, as teacher, know if you've been listened to and understood by the responses you receive. Listening and responding become the method for evaluating whether or not understanding has occurred. It is important to remember that recall is not the only necessary prerequisite to understanding. The students need to determine the intent of the message and what it means to them and then decide on a response based on an appropriate interpretation of the message.

To listen and understand requires active participation and involvement. Active listening requires that students become involved with the speaker and listen not only to the words, but also to the message. Understanding and being understood suggests a real willingness to listen and respond. The better students become at listening, the more accurate will be their interpretation of the words they hear and the responses they give those messages.

Because learning is so dependent on listening and because many students are not accomplished listeners, a listening improvement program may need to be developed in classrooms. Students can be taught effective listening strategies to improve their listening skills.

Strategies for Improving Listening

- Listen actively.
- Concentrate on what is being said.
- Distinguish between relevant and irrelevant information.
- Remove distractions.
- Show attention by body language.
- Limit your own talking.
- Don't interrupt.
- Accept other viewpoints.
- Raise questions to clarify.

Following Directions

Everyday activities provide opportunities for students to refine their abilities to follow directions. You spend much time giving directions on work assignments, textbook readings, organization of notebooks and formats for special projects. Instructions should be given briefly and clearly so that students understand exactly what they are supposed to do. Call on a student to repeat the directions if necessary. Reminders may be posted in the room when the procedures are unusual or difficult. Remind students to refer to the chart before asking for help. Fortunately, the skill for following directions is teachable and will improve with practice.

The following list assists students in listening for directions:

- Discuss the importance of following directions.
- State directions in a logical sequence.
- Minimize the number of directions.
- Give students practice sessions in following directions.
- Use language students understand.
- Encourage students to ask questions.
- Ask students to take notes.
- Follow up with written directions.

Main Ideas

Listening to get the primary thought is a common requirement in learning. Students are required to listen and read many sources in various content areas every day. When students are required to read sections in textbooks or written material, they can improve skills in identifying main ideas or emphasis areas by practicing the following:

- Paraphrase in your own words.
- Note significant words or phrases.
- Discriminate between factual statements and opinions.
- Draw inferences from facts.
- Classify information.
- Synthesize information.

You can provide a positive climate for the development of good listening skills. The following check list can be used:

Teacher Checklist for Good Listening Environment

- Am I a good model for listening?

- Do I teach listening skills?

- Do I make listening meaningful?

- Do I ask thoughtful questions?

- Do I reduce distractions?

- Do I keep information relevant?

- Do I allow students time to ask questions?

- Do I summarize content for the students?

Strategies for Improving Memory

A large amount of time in school is spent learning new material and studying that material in order to retain it for future use. Teachers use memory questions seventy percent of the time while most textbooks use memory questions as chapter summaries. With study and practice, memorization becomes easier. As students get older, they are able to remember better and pay attention longer. Students must be taught not to memorize every detail, but to be selective in what they memorize. Since students have so much material to memorize, it might be wise to make an effort to make the material interesting to them. It is easier for them to remember material they are interested in. You can develop interest in new material by being an enthusiastic and knowledgeable conveyor of information.

Students should clearly understand material before attempting memorization. Merely hearing information is not enough. Lessons should be designed to present material in small doses that can be repeated until the information is remembered. To remember a particular item, students must be taught to block out non- significant information and forget things that are irrelevant to the new material. They must form clear mental images of the concept to be memorized. Studying meaningful material and relating it to past knowledge and experience can aid in the memory process. Students who take written notes, understand and organize their work, and review periodically will learn the material more readily and retain it for longer periods of time. Many students use word associations for remembering facts. These consist of words, phrases or rhymes which are familiar to them and assist them in learning new material. These easy aids are often used by teachers for prompting students to remember material by associating two objects or ideas.

It is normal to forget unused material. Since the mind cannot remember everything, it is necessary to forget what is not relevant. Many skills not frequently used or reviewed, will be forgotten. Although time does not cause forgetting, unused information fades from immediate or short term memory. Thus, periodic reviews are essential to remembering accurately.

Concentration

The ability to concentrate varies from person to person. Students often have limited ability to control their attention and they may need help in discovering what aspects of a situation are important. Full attention to the message is required before teachers can expect students to memorize material. Attention is increased when the material and activities are interesting and when the students know they will be held responsible for what they have learned. Active involvement by students causes them to follow along and respond to questions. Don't assume that students are paying attention if they are sitting quietly and looking in the direction of whatever you want them to see or hear. However, students are capable of giving the appearance of concentrating without mentally tuning in to the information they need in order to learn. Therefore, it is important that you create situations that block out distracting details and focus attention on the task at hand. Outside noises and visual distractions often reduce concentration effectiveness. As students become older, they not only concentrate better, they also become increasingly able to tune out irrelevant information. Students can "check" themselves every time their minds wander and force themselves to focus their energies on the material. Once they've learned to keep on task, they should positively reward themselves with a snack or a short study break.

What Teachers Can Do to Improve Memory

You can use techniques for improving students' memory and concentration by implementing the following:

- Make sure students understand material.
- Identify what is important to memorize.
- Help students learn material in a meaningful way.
- Relate new learning to old learning.
- Block out distractions.
- Help students categorize material into small blocks.
- Space memorization over short time intervals.
- Suggest written notes.
- Encourage regular review of material.

Helping Teachers Speak Effectively

Teaching is a verbal activity. With words you define, clarify, interpret, explain and describe. When you have a command of the language and speak clearly and succinctly, you are more effective in the teaching process than those who speak vaguely. Knowing what kinds of experiences are likely to foster positive skills in students can help you choose activities that will have a positive effect on communication.

Speech is the most complex means of communication. A large part of communication lies in developing skill in putting together tactful and persuasive language to influence your students. Use speech to convey information to them and to ask and answer questions. Some situations consist of reporting facts, giving opinions, asking questions and responding to answers. You can use speech to directly influence the behavior of others by means of instruction through formal lectures or presentations. A common problem is the tendency to talk too much. It is also a mistake to ask questions without permitting time for the students to answer. The student with communication problems usually is confused by constant questioning and the lack of ability to answer the questions.

Speech can be personal or impersonal, concrete or abstract, friendly, interesting or boring to the audience. Informal speech consists of chit-chat and joke telling between people and is often done to relieve tension or create a positive climate. Use informal conversation prior to instruction, to relate personally to your students.

Communication involves more than merely words. Remember, you communicate warmth and feeling through your body movement and facial expressions. Students don't respond favorably to gloomy or expressionless faces. When you speak, look at your students and have a friendly smile on your face. Facial expressions tell whether you are strained or relaxed, eager or bored. Smile at the students as your eyes sweep across your audience. A friendly face and a happy smile tells them that you are interested in them. A frozen smile or frown can express negative meaning. By being stiff and unnatural, you create uneasiness. Say what you have to say in the way which is easiest and most natural for you. Each statement you make is received by your audience as favorable or unfavorable. If your students react unfavorably to you, they will not respond to you, or worse, they will stop listening to you. If, on the other hand, they receive what you say positively, they will be motivated to be supportive towards you and tend to actively respond to your comments. If you communicate confidence to your students, they will be less inclined to be critical or hostile.

When speaking to groups of students, you will have to adapt you language to fit the audience. Talk to students at their levels of speech, rather than using words that might be difficult for them to understand. If you use ambiguous words, the students will simply wonder what you are talking about, and after a while, stop listening. Take caution to define vague words. You can define words and put the words into context. By putting the words into context, you define the way you want the student to understand the word. Use words that reveal sincerity and ones that are simple, definite and specific. This can be accomplished by using pleasant words that don't offend. Words that ridicule and criticize are all destructive and will lead to poor communication. Words to avoid include: lazy, dumb, no, cheat, below average or fail. Avoid using slang. Use attractive words which express the exact meaning you want.

There are many ways to keep your audience alert. Maintain a positive climate and strive to stimulate the students by following these suggestions:

Ways to Keep Your Students Awake

1. Know your subject matter.
2. Say what you mean in a logical way.
3. Use understandable language.
4. Make your explanations clear and concise.
5. Use visual aids when appropriate.
6. Keep your eye on the students.
7. Speak up.
8. Be enthusiastic.
9. Be brief.

You can measure the success of your presentation not only by the students' reacting as you want, but also by their reactions to what you say. If they are attentive and ask appropriate questions, you have been successful.

Voice Quality

A pleasant voice is a great asset and sets the instructional tone. There is no magic formula for a good voice. Students respond well to teachers who speak clearly and pleasantly, not too fast or too slow, not too loudly or too softly. The speed and volume with which you speak are important. A pleasant voice minimizes confusion because each word is enunciated clearly. A well modulated voice projects well, without excessive loudness. When you speak to students, you must project forcefully. Failure to project the voice may make the words less effective. Pitch, loudness and rate of delivery convey emotional meanings to the learners. Use simple, straightforward language and talk at a moderate rate in order to be understood by all. Pick out someone in the group and project your voice to that point. Your tone then will carry to the rest of the students. A loud, shrill, piercing voice detracts from the message and the listener "turns off" to the words spoken. Teachers who have command of the language and who speak distinctly are more effective than those who speak vaguely.

Each time you talk, you share parts of your personality. Some teachers are dynamic enough to convey their energy to the students. Others manage their words so well that they ignite students' interest. An imaginative, well thought out class presentation can arouse and captivate your audience. You can communicate interest and enthusiasm by raising your voice, increasing the rate of presentation and using many action and descriptive words. Disinterest is communicated by an even pitch or monotone and through a slow, boring tempo. Most people unconsciously emphasize the words they want to get across when conversing. For example, you can select the main idea and say it louder or pause before and after key words. When speaking, be deliberate, crisp, and forceful and your audience will enjoy listening to you.

Many people consider a good voice a gift, but voice quality can be developed to display attractive qualities. Learn what the normal, natural tone and pitch of your voice are, then take time to practice speaking naturally. All public speakers need to analyze speech habits regularly. The sound of your voice isn't carried to you in the same way as other sounds.

53

You hear your voice differently than others hear it. One of the best ways to study and improve the quality of your speech is by making a tape recording of your voice.

Tape twenty minutes of a class situation in which you are interacting with the students. You may wish to make two recordings. The first one would be a formal lecture or presentation. The second one would be an impromptu situation where you are interacting informally with the students, either individually or in a group. Listen to the tapes and note word and sentence patterns, vocabulary and grammar. Ask yourself the following questions:

1. Am I repeating word patterns?
2. Is what I say interesting?
3. Am I using correct, Standard English?
4. Does my voice sound monotonous?
5. Am I using unnecessary words and sentences?
6. Is my voice loud and clear?
7. Do I talk too much?
8. What can I do to improve my voice?

No one can improve your speech except you yourself. Practice exercises can be of great help. These questions serve as prompts for presentations. Each time you make a note of how you talk, you develop your own speech consciousness. You'll begin to pick out words you mumble or pronounce incorrectly. You'll hear "ask" pronounced "awsk" or "ast." Don't irritate your students by repeating over and over words such as "uh," "unh," "er-uh." Instead of using these sounds, pause occasionally then continue talking in a clear manner without hesitation. Frequent checks of your speech will sharpen your own pronunciation. In listening to yourself speak, you will recognize repetition of words such as "yes," "you know," "because," "well," "again" and so on. Repetitive word patterns are easy to correct by eliminating the identified words in your speech. Listening to yourself and becoming aware of errors of grammar and pronunciation will help you improve your speech. Research has shown that analyzing your speech will aid not only in the refinement of speech patterns, but in the development of the range and depth of your voice.

Distracting Gestures

All of us have been in an audience when the speaker made distracting gestures throughout a speech. These are movements of the body and limbs that the speaker seems unaware of. They distract from communication because they take attention away from the speech. They make the audience uncomfortable and unable to concentrate on the message. One way to become aware of your gestures is to video tape a group presentation and view it privately. When reviewing the video tape, carefully note the distracting mannerisms and design a plan to gain control of the movement or gesture. Consciously work toward minimizing distracting movements and become more confident in your instructional presentations. Frequent distracting gestures include:

Continuous blinking	Biting lips
Twitching eye brows	Licking lips
Tapping fingers	Pulling ears
Scratching head	Cracking knuckles
Clearing throat	Swallowing repeatedly

Nonverbal Communication

Too often we think of communication only in terms of verbal communication, yet the nonverbal aspects are just as important as the verbal messages we give. One function of body movement and gestures is to amplify speech. When we express ourselves in words, our whole body reacts. We give several thousand different signals through our gestures and body language. All of us are fairly skilled in observing others' nonverbal language. However, although body language is easy to observe, it may be difficult to interpret. Facial expressions, hand gestures, body position and even clothing provide clues about a person's attitudes and behaviors. Nonverbal communication is a continuous process. Just because you've stopped talking, body clues do not "shut down." Your students continue to observe movements and gestures. Although these nonverbal clues provide continuous useful information, they often are misinterpreted or misunderstood. There are many elements of nonverbal communication. The following list encompasses many ways in which you send messages.

Silence	Hairstyle	Appearance
Posture	Lip movement	Timing
Dress	Eye movement	Positioning
Touch	Physical movement	Facial expression

People tend to display happiness or disappointment through their nonverbal facial expressions of smiles and frowns. Students often interpret your emotional state from a quick glance at your facial expression. Therefore, if you want to give the impression that you're happy and eager, "put on a happy face". Other facial expressions convey many meanings: anger, fear, boredom, disgust and lack of interest. Since students depend so much on facial expressions for the meaning of the message, be aware of their importance and make sure your facial expressions reinforce and compliment the verbal message.

Effective speakers are very conscious of bodily movements. Gesturing is a principal movement which communicates a wide variety of meanings. Hand gestures can emphasize and add meaning to important words. They can add expressiveness to your presentation or can distract from it. When not using your hands, let them hang naturally. Hands should not be stuck in pockets or folded unnaturally across the chest. Hands should not be used to straighten clothing, rub noses, or smooth hair. It is difficult to identify the most effective gestures. Speakers use the specific gestures they find comfortable. Although there are many gestures, the best gesture is the natural one. Feet should be planted firmly on the ground and balance should be maintained with body weight evenly distributed on both feet. If you are comfortable moving around the room, be careful not to tramp heavily over an uncarpeted area. Excessive pacing and movement are irritating and distracting.

Physical Appearance

Personal relationships can be encouraged or discouraged by our physical appearance. Clothing, makeup and hair styling serve to form first impressions probably more than other aspects of nonverbal language. Research studies found that physical attractiveness and dress of the teacher is one of the most important variables in interpersonal relationships. Clothes create images of who we are and how we feel about ourselves. Your type of dress plays an important role in forming first impressions as well as creating a willingness to cooperate. The more formally attired teachers are perceived as being the most knowledgeable and the most desirable teachers.

Research done by Molloy (1977) found that color, pattern and cut of teachers' clothes affect attitudes, attention spans, and conduct of high school and junior high school students. You need to carefully choose what you wear when facing students. Male teachers should select clothes such as suits, sports jackets and slacks, or slacks with tailored shirts. Female teachers should wear skirted suits, tailored dresses, skirts and blouses, or pantsuits. If teachers are untidy or wear unsuitable clothes, they may ruin the effect of what they say. Improving your appearance is easy and makes you more distinctive and personable. Good clothes, worn well, increase your confidence and gives a stronger, more positive impression. Dress also makes a difference in the perception of teachers by students. Therefore, teachers can enhance effectiveness by improving their physical appearance.

Effective Use of Media

Using audiovisual media will effectively enhance your presentation if you use it appropriately. Likewise, poor use of media detracts from the presentation and can irritate the students. A good, attractive visual aid will help the listeners focus on the lesson. In order for visual aids to work, they must help illustrate your point. The visual aid should be shown only when you are making the same point it does. Media give visual as well as auditory clues. Because there are many ways to teach subject matter, you may want to use visual aids to reinforce and enliven your presentation or illustrate important points. There are a variety of visual aids available to teachers. They include films, video tapes, audio tapes, laser discs, computers, slides, film strips, transparencies, flip charts, robots, chalkboards and posters.

Selection and use of the media is important. Once you have made a decision on the format of the lesson, you can decide if the addition of media would be beneficial. Once the media is selected, the following points should be checked:

1. Is everyone positioned to see the screen?
2. Can everyone hear the audio tape?
3. Does the machinery work? Do you have spare bulbs? Do you have an extension cord?
4. Do you know how to operate the equipment?
5. Can the printed material be read from the back of the room?
6. Does the media add to your presentation?

Dealing with a Student Audience

Experienced teachers have many ways to change student moods and behaviors and to get the group to feel more positive about the class work. When students arrive, you might want to talk informally with them. Students often enter the room engrossed in their own thoughts and concerns that may vary significantly from the topic of discussion. These ideas may interfere with the students' ability to concentrate attention on the message. Listening to what students say can give you clues to their moods and to other interests they may have. If they have not been assigned seats, most students, when entering the room, will seek out their friends or acquaintances to sit with. Students sit with their friends to communicate and establish relationships with them. Social interaction is a normal and important behavior, but often gets in the way of effective learning. Your attempts to control this behavior often cause problems in communication between students and the teacher. Designate short periods of time, either before or during class, for students to interact with each other. You may want to regularly change seating patterns to encourage different social interactions. Changing the seating will increase group cohesiveness and usually will cause the students to interact more positively with each other. Students are more likely stay "on task" when they are not concentrating and performing for classmates.

Once instruction begins, you, as well as other students, will be distracted if students talk or walk around while you are speaking. Disruptive talking often takes place because students do not understand your directions. When you are not clear, students are likely to become confused and ask one another for directions. You will be able to diminish excessive talking by developing instructional plans which are clear and stimulating to the students. There are many ways to handle this kind of behavior. You may want to ignore the behavior as long as possible, increase your volume and go on. Or, you may send eye messages to the students by looking directly at them, pausing and then continuing with the discussions. Another technique is to use body movements to position yourself in direct proximity to the distracting student. Being able to easily walk around the room makes this an effective technique. The group often disciplines its own members by telling one another to "quiet down" or "stop talking." If the distraction gets bad enough, just stop speaking and confront the situation. Asking a student to "sit down" usually works. If the distraction continues, you may want to inform the students that the noise level is bothering you and give them an opportunity to quiet down.

Non-Standard English

At the present time, there are some million standard and non- standard speakers in the country with a variety of formal and informal speech patterns. A large number of students come to schools speaking languages other then standard English. Language differs in the meaning attached to words, pronunciations, and word patterns. Effective communication requires, to some extent, the active promotion of a standard language.

Speakers of standard English may fail to adjust listening habits and may make value judgments. Several educational studies have shown that students who speak in non-standard English tend to be negatively perceived by teachers. On the other hand, students who speak without dialect and who display good speech styles are rated as better students, identified as more self confident and received better grades. (Howell and Vetter, 1985)

Accent and dialect often identify geographical, as well as educational background. The greater the formal education,the more likely we are to use the standard variety of language. Speech also reveals range of vocabulary and range of topic areas we are able to talk about and understand. Since most teachers use standard English when teaching, using "good" English is associated with formal learning.

You can emphasize the importance of using standard reading and writing as communication tools. You also can encourage students to talk and listen to each other in order to use and hear words in a variety of situations. Students who use non-standard English can read and listen to standard English without difficulty. They comprehend and remember standard English as well as they do their own dialect. Student's verbal fluency and communication effectiveness can be enhanced by providing opportunities for them to hear and use the language correctly.

Research seems to suggest that students who do not speak standard English are likely to develop low expectations and negative attitudes in teachers. While some teachers are willing to tolerate non-standard English to avoid discouraging the student, most teachers show greater admiration for the students who dress well and communicate in standard English.

Summary

This chapter discussed the communication strategies that may be utilized by teachers to develop positive rapport with their students. Communication involves more than merely words. To be an effective communicator, the students must be able to process the words you say and assign meaning to them. Communication is the exchange of information from one person to another. It is talking to each other and sharing descriptions, explanations, events, ideas and feelings. When we actively involve ourselves in communication, we understand and see the world as the other person sees it.

When teachers strive to improve communication skills such as listening, understanding, memory and concentration, significant academic gains can be accomplished. Students learn the importance of communication skills by positive interactions with teachers and peers. All students benefit from the communication strategies described in this chapter.

5

Preparing for Homework

The type of homework assignments continues to be a controversial subject for teachers. Teachers still debate about the type of homework to assign. The debate ranges from teachers who insist on assigning regular practice and enrichment type homework, to assigning homework that prepares students for classwork. Making homework effective can begin with the efforts of committed teachers who design worthwhile homework. All teachers agree that the quality of the homework is the most important factor when assigning out of class work. Effective assignments promote learning by helping students master specific skills through practice in using the skills and by requiring the students to go beyond the skills and apply the information to new situations. Preparation homework helps prepare students for material they will learn in class situations. Properly constructed homework will review concepts, prepare students for new concepts and extend the students' knowledge to the real world. Students should expect assignments which have clearly defined objectives, which support classroom instruction, and which reevaluate to reward mastery.

Assigning Homework

The following guidelines for constructing homework assignments will increase the likelihood of effective learning taking place.

1. Clarify homework assignments by making assignments on a weekly basis. Encourage students to use a weekly assignment sheet to keep track of their assignments and remind them about due dates. A sample assignment sheet might look like the following.

Math

M	Pg. 101 1 - 8
T	Pg. 120 1,3,5,7,9,
W	Pg. 126 10 - 20
TH	Review pages 101-126
F	Test on Chapter 4

2. Make sure students understand the assignments and can complete them independently. Keep directions short and simple.
3. Try to limit homework to one hour.
4. Ensure that all students have the materials needed to complete the assignments.
5. Assign high interest work whenever possible. Attempt to personalize assignments.
6. Reinforce assignments in class by reviewing materials covered in the assignments.
7. Give students regular feedback by making comments on the work.
8. Grade all homework.
9. Assign homework as extra credit to help students bring up their grades.
10. Make sure students know how the homework grades fit into their final grade.

Organizing Study Environments in School

Supervised study is used in many schools today. The classroom or library provides effective places for study under the supervision of a teacher. Many schools today use supervised study to assist students with specific assignments and allow them opportunities to complete unfinished work. It is important that students who request academic assistance are provided with favorable work environments. Educators have known for a long time that the physical environment has a direct influence on behavior. Behaviors are reactions to the environments in which they take place. It is also known that the physical environment has profound effects on individual school behavior and on the rate of educational progress. People adopt continuously and actively to their surroundings by changing both themselves and their environment. The physical and spatial aspects of a learning environment communicate to the students what the teacher expects to happen in the specified space.

How can you, as teacher, provide an environment that is conducive to learning? The research supports providing individual and personalized study environments to enhance learning. Organizing work spaces for independent study requires taking into account furniture and furniture arrangement, lighting, materials and noise factors.

Furniture

Providing study areas in a library or media center requires a close look at the physical layout of the room and the furniture within the room. Study spaces should be arranged to allow for efficient use of space, accessible materials and supplies and individual work centers. Each study environment should be responsive to and appropriate for individual students. The arranged physical environment can support instruction by complementing and reinforcing teaching strategies. The furniture can be arranged in the study areas in such a way that it supports quiet study. The placement of furniture in strategic locations will stimulate students to work independently to complete homework assignments. There may be things in the study environment you cannot change or can change only temporarily. If you want to make the physical environment more conducive to individual study, furniture can be rearranged to provide small study areas. Work areas should not face windows close to busy streets or noisy playgrounds. Study centers should be in places where environment noises are at the lowest possible decibel level.

Work areas should be positioned so they allow for maximum privacy. This privacy can be achieved by establishing a barrier to sight or sound. There is little opportunity for privacy in large rooms in schools. A physical change in a classroom or library that provides for some privacy is the provision of small, isolated work areas designated for individual study. This might be accomplished by seating students in isolated areas around the room.

While assisting students, you will want to have areas designated for small group work. Space large enough for groups of three or four encourages cooperation and attention and allows you to work on specific skills with a groups of three or four students. Designating areas for working with students in small groups is also necessary. One way to do this is to arrange chairs around a table that is positioned away from the individual work areas. It is important that all students have individual areas to practice the skills they learned. While the space needs to be large enough for students to have within their reach all of the books and resource material they need to complete assignments, the space should also be small enough to remain private and quiet.

Noise

Noise is any sound that is unpleasant, annoying or disruptive of performance. Noise has different effects on different people. Many students are surrounded by noise in their environments which they are unable to control. The noise might include street noise, playground noise, television noise, radio or stereo noise. Success in completing homework assignments is influenced by the quietness of the study environment.

Noise, during study time distracts students more when conditions are crowded and dense. The larger the number of people, the more likely they are to be distracted by people and the noises they make. If students are in environments where noise is a major factor for extended periods of time, academic performance will likely be affected. Research indicates that the presence of noise may have the following significant effects:

1. Noise contributes to lack of concentration.
2. Noise affects comprehension in reading.
3. High noise levels cause students to make more mistakes.

Noise abatement is usually necessary when students are involved in study sessions. Fortunately, in study assistance centers, you have some control over the noise in the environment. When you create quiet and appropriate study areas, noise and disruptions decrease. Although much has been written concerning the necessity for quiet study environments, many students continue to study while listening to radios and stereos. Encourage students not to bring these items to study sessions. When students have concentrated reading assignments, additional efforts should be made to provide for study in quieter places.

Noise detracts depending upon the activity required by the students. A high noise level in a science laboratory is not as distracting as a high noise level in a testing situation. When assisting students in a library or classroom, attempt to maintain a quiet environment. When you minimize noise levels during study times, the quality of work increases.

Heating and Lighting

People tend to prefer temperatures between 68 degrees and 75 degrees F. For that reason, most school systems operate temperatures in classrooms of 70 degrees F. When the temperature of a room is excessively high, students get uncomfortably warm and have a tendency to work at a somewhat slower rate. When the room temperature is excessively low, students become uncomfortably cold and quickly lose interest in class work. If you do not have control over the temperature of a very warm room, suggest to students that they remove coats or sweaters and sit away from the sunlight.

Visual tasks such as reading and writing require an adequate level of illumination for efficient performance. Reading and writing assignments often require prolonged and close attention to the printed page. Students are often required to read small and large print on the same page and visually change from matte paper to glossy paper in one study session. Because of the differences in types of paper and print, the lighting system should consist of direct lighting.

A direct lighting system is one in which the light is directed downward. Table or floor lamps are preferred for study purposes in a direct lighting system. When students are studying at school, the lighting should be consistent and without glare. Lighting should be evenly distributed on the study area. Most classrooms and libraries have fluorescent lighting which is diffused and ideal for study purposes. However, fluorescent lighting, when it has been used for long periods of time, may begin to flicker. This causes shadows on the study area and detracts from the flow of the light. Therefore, it is important to watch for flickering lights and correct them immediately.

Materials

Effective learning requires practice using the skills taught. It is important for you to provide students with opportunities to interface with support materials which reinforce the skills taught. Students should have available the books they will need to complete their assignments. If they do not have the texts available, you might want to provide additional textbooks for their use. Resource books and materials should be kept within easy reach. Materials such as pencils, papers or books should be provided for students and be kept in designated work areas. When you keep support materials in visible reach, near or in work spaces, students are more likely to use them. If you do not provide pencils and paper for students, students will waste time locating these necessary supplies.

When you place frequently used materials in an isolated place, students walking to the centralized location often waste time talking or interrupting other students on the way. Students who need academic assistance are often looking for excuses not to complete assignments and tend to waste time. The amount of time spent getting material often takes up more time than the work itself.

Conversely, when support materials are hidden from view or located in hard-to-get-to spots, students tend not to use them. Pencils, paper, and chalk should be arranged in boxes and placed on designated study tables. When study sessions are over, these boxes can be stored for future use.

If media or visual aids are used, students should be as close to the media as possible to enhance visual acuity. Other support resources, such as calculators and computers, should be readily accessible and close to electrical outlets.

Managing Instructional Assistance Time

The amount of time you spend assisting students will vary from day to day. It is important that you maximize the study time spent with students by minimizing interruptions and distractions.

When attempting to maximize the time spent helping students, start the assistance process as quickly as possible. If students are scheduled to come to you for help at 3:35, begin the help sessions as close to 3:35 as possible. Students who come to you after the regular school day or at a designated time during the school day, often come in a loud, chaotic manner. Show them how to organize themselves and streamline their tasks and then have them practice until they begin work quickly, efficiently and quietly. Encourage students to come to you with the materials needed to complete their work. Time should not be wasted looking for books and sharpening pencils. To be an effective study assistant, you must ensure that students not only have their books and supplies, but are paying attention to what they have to do. Before you begin the help session, explain what you are going to do and how you are going to do it. One way to improve attention is to tell the students the specific goals students will be working toward. Attempt to provide a supportive environment that encourages students to ask for help so they can receive the academic assistance they need.

To minimize student interruptions, inform students that you will assist each of them and suggest that they begin work on their assignments until you are able to help them. Be sure to get to each of them as quickly as possible. Allocate time to various students on the basis of the degree of assistance required. You might have to spend only a short period of time helping one student get started on an assignment, while you might have to spend a much longer period of time with another. Teach students to wait their turns and not interrupt you while you are working with other students. You might encourage students to raise their hands when they need help. Recognize their raised hands immediately before they become noisy and disruptive. Students who need academic help should not have to wait for extended periods of time to get help. When they have to wait, even for a few minutes, valuable learning and teaching time is wasted. Thus, to develop on-task behavior and increase learning, encourage students to ask for assistance when needed, but suggest that they continue working until you get to them.

If a small group of students experiences difficulty in the same subject area, have them work together until you can assist them. Be sure you pace your time so that all students can get your help quickly and as needed. In an attempt to manage time more efficiently, you may tend to rush the students. Don't be too quick to help. Once the problem has been identified, allow students to familiarize themselves with the assignment by completing all the items they are able to do. Suggest to the students that they work quickly and efficiently. When students learn not to interrupt you while you are assisting someone else, they'll learn to respect you and the time you spend assisting them with their assignments.

Be available to the students when they are working independently and encourage them to ask questions or request additional help when they need it. When students are wrong, help them correct their mistakes. Continue to assist them until they get the correct answers, but do so in a positive way.

Monitoring students' progress and correcting their work are important aides to learning. As you circulate among the students and provide individual assistance, make sure they are progressing by quickly checking their work. Students who are having academic difficulties need immediate feedback that tells them they are completing the assignments correctly. You want them to feel good about what they are doing and to know that they are doing their work correctly. You do not want them to continue practicing a skill the wrong way. Begin by circulating among students who are having serious difficulties. In starting with these students, you will make sure that you have sufficient time to assist them. When circulating among students, it is easy to catch small mistakes and correct them. You may also identify students who need additional assistance. Immediately schedule longer periods of time to work with these students. You can then assign a small number of similar items for them to practice.

Each time you stop at a study area, be sure to praise the students for their efforts. Recognize their correct answers and evidence of progress by giving a check mark, star or verbal praise. Incorrect answers can be pointed out verbally or by placing a short pencil line next to the item. When the student corrects the work, the mark can be turned into a check mark or covered with a sticker.

Many students will come to help sessions with more work than can be accomplished in one study session. Forty to fifty minutes is an appropriate block of study time for most students. Work out a schedule with the students where they can separate the assignments into blocks of time. Together decide on what will be the first priority and what can be accomplished in the next week and write it down in a weekly schedule. Do not encourage the students to cover too much material in a short study session. Teach them how to manage their time in such a way that they can prioritize their assignments and realistically schedule their completion.

There are several ways you as a teacher can manage your time with students. The following checklist should assist you in time management.

Teacher Time Management Checklist

		Yes	No
1.	Do you quickly identify problem areas?	___	___
2.	Do you explain to the students how you are going to help them?	___	___
3.	Do you begin assisting students immediately?	___	___
4.	Do you give students time to ask questions and respond to your questions?	___	___
5.	Do you manage your assistance time so that you are available to all students?	___	___

6. Do you help students work efficiently, stay on task, and improve their work habits?   ____ ____

7. Are you in control of interruptions?   ____ ____

Taking Good Notes

There are several ways students can become more efficient during class time that will assist them later when completing homework and studying for tests. Teaching students to take good notes and to underline important facts is useful to them. Because students have large amounts of new information to process each day, taking good notes is necessary to assist the students in learning the material. The techniques for recognizing significant points of a lecture require students to become active listeners. They need to listen for main ideas and write them down for future study. Good notetaking is a valuable skill for all students to learn. Listening to information to select the main ideas and then writing them down in condensed form helps students make sense of the material later. Notetaking increases listening skills and helps students concentrate on the important points of lectures.

Students should be encouraged to come to class prepared with a notebook in which to take notes. Since much of what is said in class will be covered on exams, students must write down all important information. It is easy for students to forget key points of lectures. If they don't write down the ideas that were emphasized. The first thing you can do is give them practice sessions in notetaking. Reserve a few class sessions to assist students in effective notetaking techniques. To help them remember key points, give them visual clues throughout the lesson. Prior to class lectures, write key words or phrases on the chalkboard or prepare class handouts summarizing the material covered in class. This information should be short and pertinent to class presentations. Throughout the presentation, refer to the printed material and suggest to the students that they copy all information written on the chalkboard or circle key words on the printed page. When you have not prepared written material, encourage students to jot down specific key words or main phrases they heard you say. In the beginning, you will probably have to tell them what to write. A few practice sessions will help them practice writing down appropriate words and phrases. Teach them to pay special attention to words which the teacher repeats or says louder than other words. Phrases such as the following usually give students auditory clues to important ideas:

Remember this. . .

Let me repeat myself. . .

This is important. . .

Let's review this material. . .

Jot down this idea. . .

You can encourage students to take effective notes that will aid them in learning important information. It will also assist them in completing homework assignments and studying for exams. When reviewing effective notetaking strategies, the following list might be taken into consideration:

Strategies for Good Notetaking

1. Come to class prepared with paper and pencils to write legible notes.
2. Take notes on all class lectures and presentations.
3. Copy all material written on the chalkboard.
4. Read all printed material distributed in class. Highlight main ideas.
5. Write down all key words and phrases that indicate important points.
6. Use word abbreviations and shortened forms of words.
7. Summarize and clarify notes immediately after class.
8. Read and review notes regularly.
9. When studying, recite in your own words the information in notes.

Underlining

Underlining is a popular technique used when reading textbooks or other printed material. It is similar to notetaking in that key words are underlined. Underlining is usually done when students own their own textbooks or when teachers distribute printed material such as journal articles, chapters of books, or news clips. Unfortunately, students usually underline too much; many of them underline almost every line. When this is done, the underlined sections will lose their significance when the students reread the sections for future study. Rather than underlining too many sentences and phrases, encourage students to use different colored markers to highlight main ideas, new terms, and summary statements. Circling key words or jotting down notes in the margins makes the material more meaningful. Students can devise their own symbols such as stars for key words or checks for enumerations of lists. Encourage students to review underlined material and organize their notes when studying.

Establishing Learning Environments in the Home

Creating appropriate study space in the home is essential to maintaining good study habits. When study environments are aesthetically pleasing, students are more likely to respond positively to homework assignments. A home study environment should be made to look as attractive as possible.

Encourage students to designate a specific place to study in their homes. A learning environment in the home can be a private area in a designated room. A room without a lot of noise, movement and activity is preferred for effective study. When deciding on a study area, suggest to the students that it be separate from noisy areas. Sounds from televisions, radios, stereos and other household sounds need to be avoided when selecting a study area. Specific parts of a home may be more conducive to study during different parts of the day. A kitchen may be an ideal place to study after dinner, but an inappropriate place to study in the afternoon hours because of the activity and noise in the room. Distractions interrupt concentration. Since students listen and concentrate on what is important to them, sounds from a television or telephone can interrupt concentration on work assignments. The elimination or minimization of distractions is necessary in a study area since interference with concentration will generate poor study habits.

A study area can be a desk in a bedroom or it can be a table in the kitchen. When students have their own bedrooms, the study area should be a desk or table in their bedroom. It students do not have access to a desk or designated room, a kitchen table can be used effectively. The study desk should be cleared of unnecessary objects and be placed facing a wall. If students sit at a kitchen table to study, they should position themselves in such a way as to minimize visual and auditory distractions. Facing toward the wall will usually accomplish this. Beds, soft chairs and floors do not provide good study areas. It is too easy to fall asleep or become distracted when study is taking place while lounging on a bed or a sofa.

After students have selected an area for study, comfortable seating is critical for prolonged periods of time. Remember, most students have homework assignments to complete four days a week and those assignments usually take one hour to complete. If a seat is too high or too deep, it causes pain to the legs or back. An overly soft seat may cause the students to sleep, rather than study. An overly hard seat is uncomfortable for extended periods of time. Once students are seated comfortably, encourage them to have the materials they will need within easy reach when seated. Storage locations for frequently used materials such as pencils, paper and books should be within normal seated reach or stored in such a place where students will have easy access to them.

The desk or table in the study area should be positioned to provide for maximizing lighting. Normal levels of light increase visual efficiency. Poor levels of light cause eye fatigue. Lighting should be evenly distributed on the surface of the desk. The light should not shine directly in the eyes or produce a glare on the printed pages. Fluorescent lamps are a popular and improved lighting system used in many desk lamps. New design improvements have produced warm, soft lamps which reduce glare. Although most desk lamps are made with fluorescent bulbs, lamps which provide for even distribution of light are just as effective.

Communication with Parents

When teachers make an effort to communicate with parents, the parents usually become strong supporters, not only of the teacher, but of the school. All parents want their children to learn. They have a right to know what their children are doing in school and how well they are doing it. They want to know what is expected of their children and many parents want to know how they can help. You should clearly communicate to parents various aspects of the program: how instruction is given, how students are expected to behave and how progress will be communicated. When problems occur, parents need to become aware of the problems and participate in plans to correct them.

There are many ways to communicate with parents:

Class newsletters   Special events
Open House Programs   Written comments
Conferences   Handbooks
Classroom visits   Class parties

Successful communication requires regular and continuous news about the classroom, especially about the achievement of the students and their progress in school. Continuity between home and school provides an important support system for today's families.

Tips for Parents

1. Encourage your child to schedule a specific homework study time each day. Help him remain on schedule by suggesting that he get started on time. Parents should help their child decide on a quiet, comfortable place to study.

2. Parents need to remember not to do the homework for the child. It is the child's assignment, not the parent's. Be there to assist him with any questions he may have, but don't complete the assignments for him. When he is wrong, let him know, but do it in a way that will not discourage him. Remember to reward efforts with praise, smiles and hugs.

3. Work with your child to decide on specific goals to work toward. A goal for one child might be to complete a term paper by Friday. A goal for another might be to work towards completing homework within one hour each evening. If reasonable goals are set, and agreed upon, they are more likely to be accomplished.

4. Instead of ordering or threatening, help your child improve his ability to concentrate by praising him when he begins or ends an assignment. Punishment tends to curtail curiosity and often prevents children from learning appropriately. Verbal praise, a sticker, or a treat are all appropriate rewards and should be given often by parents. Praising success will help your child develop responsible behavior.

5. If problems occur, discuss them with your child. Try not to over react to situations. The homework assignments may be too hard or too easy. If problems continue, you may want to meet with the teacher to discuss the specific problem.

6. Look over your child's completed work each day. While your encouragement is important, it is your child's responsibility to complete the assignments correctly. Ask questions when you are unsure of answers and insist on neatness and accuracy. Let your child know that you are interested and supportive of his efforts.

7. Encourage your child to bring homework home from school each day. Since most homework is graded by the teacher, your child will not get credit for homework that is not turned in. You may want to have a special homework folder to help your child keep track of his finished work.

8. Locate the closest public library and secure a library card. Visit the library with your child on a regular basis.

9. It is important for your child to do the best he can in school. These "Tips for Parents" will help you and your child make learning a rewarding experience.

Managing Student Study Time

One of the most important study skills is knowing how to budget time. When students become organized and learn to budget their time, they will waste less time. By learning to manage time, students will have more time for study, play and other out of school activities.

Creating schedules helps students make better use of their time. A weekly homework schedule will give them ideas on how to plan for completing their work. For example, if Joel has a science test on Friday, he may not be able to go to the football game on Thursday unless he studies for the test Wednesday night and Friday morning. When weekly schedules are made, students can make sure that they have scheduled enough study time before the night of the test to accommodate unexpected situations.

Help students devise a weekly study schedule to assist them with staying up-to-date on assignments and course work. Study schedules provide for a systematic, regular study plan that will develop good work habits. A weekly schedule should be divided in blocks of time for each day of the week. The blocks of time can be one hour blocks or two hour blocks of time. Study time should be scheduled for each day of the week. Weekend days are often used for long term projects or reports. When scheduling study times, students must take into consideration the dates of tests and the dates assignments are due in various classes. When assignments are given, students should write the assignment on the weekly schedule and allow sufficient study time for each assignment. The most important and difficult subjects should be scheduled first and at a time when students are most alert. For many students, that time may be early in the morning. For others, it may be late afternoon or early evening. Difficult subjects may require more study time and should be scheduled in larger blocks of time than less difficult subjects. Monitoring study times will allow students to adjust the schedule when unexpected events occur. Encourage students to schedule assignments to be completed ahead of time to allow for unexpected last minute problems.

Scheduling short review times before specific class sessions will help students reconsider information that will be discussed in class. Several study periods for upcoming tests should be scheduled a week in advance, and a couple of short review periods should be scheduled the day before the test. Cramming large amounts of information the night before the test is not an effective study technique. A weekly study schedule helps students make efficient use of available time and helps them gain control of their homework assignments. A written schedule forces students to study daily and on a regular basis to eliminate cramming for tests or not completing assignments.

Weekly Study Schedule

TIME	Monday	Tuesday	Wednesday	Thursday	Friday	Saturday	Sunday
7:00-9:00							
9:00-11:00							
1:00-3:00							
3:00-5:00							
5:00-7:00							
7:00-9:00							
9:00-11:00							
LONG TERM PROJECTS							
DUE DATES							

Getting Started

Teach students to avoid procrastination. Try to help them tackle the tough assignments first, since their energy levels are higher when they first begin the homework.

Teach them to spend a few minutes each evening getting organized. They should decide which subject to complete first, and then order the remaining subjects according to difficulty level. Each time they complete an assignment, have them put it away before they get out the next assignment. Encourage them to keep all the materials they will need to use to complete assignments. Much time can be wasted when materials are not ready or accessible.

The following procedures can be used to give students guidance about using their time wisely:

1. Read the directions of the assignment before getting started. If they are not clear, read them again out loud or to someone else. Paraphrasing often helps in understanding.
2. Review notes before attempting to answer homework assignments. If there are questions to answer at the end of a chapter, it is likely that the answers will be found in their handwritten notes. When all questions are completed, review the answers and correct spelling and grammar. Notes provide short summaries of important information in texts. Encourage students to copy notes that are written on the chalkboard. They should also pay attention to BOLD FACE type in textbooks. Figures and diagrams should also be reviewed and related to homework assignments.
3. Complete all homework assignments in the scheduled time. Remind students to go back and review their completed work to ensure that it is done accurately.
4. Encourage students to obtain a notebook or folder to save their notes and outlines. The information becomes beneficial when studying for tests.

Time Saving Tips

1. Schedule time wisely. Schedule assignments according to due dates.
2. Prepare for study sessions in advance. Prepare a weekly study schedule.
3. Monitor study times. Prioritize homework assignments. Complete major assignments first. Improve work habits. Change if necessary.
4. Find a quiet place to study. Avoid interruptions.
5. Take good notes. Review and write them in your own words.
6. Get organized. Know what you have to do and what materials you need in order to complete assignments. Don't waste time.
7. Work cooperatively on group projects. Ask others to help you.
8. Make decisions quickly. Decide fast what is important.
9. Overcome procrastination. Start now.
10. Finish things immediately.

Managing Stress

Students today are experiencing more stress in their everyday lives than ever before. Stress, which occurs when a person's self image doesn't match what is actually in his life, is a growing concern for students of all ages. There are many expected and unexpected difficult occurrences that happen every day in the lives of students. Students often become frustrated and disappointed with school and homework assignments. Although some stress is positive and pushes us to reach established goals in life, most stress has long term negative effects. Many students experience excessive stress created by achievement and productivity demands. Stress causes tension when which can have ill effects on our bodies and our reactions to things that happen to us. You, as teachers, can help students react to problem situations in a positive way by suggesting ways that they can cope with their stress. When students learn to cope with their stress situations and learn to control their reaction to them, they can act in a more rational manner.

The following hints will help students minimize stress in their lives:

1. Get plenty of rest, exercise and eat healthy foods.
2. Change daily routines. Completing homework assignments at different times during the week will offer variety.
3. Balance work with play. Set aside time each day to relax and have fun.
4. Set realistic goals. Monitor and adjust them regularly.
5. Avoid overloading your day. Schedule reasonable deadlines.
6. If you are unable to complete classwork and homework assignments, talk with the teacher. Ask for help.
7. Take frequent breaks while doing long assignments.
8. Be yourself. Learn to understand your shortcomings and your strengths.
9. Positively reinforce yourself. Be good to yourself.

The first thing you can do as teacher is to help students discover the source of their problems. Causes for stress in students might include: excessive homework assignments, poor grades, inability to complete work, poor health and poor self concept. Once students have identified the source of their stress, they can develop a plan for change. A definite, well thought out plan will help eliminate or reduce stress sources.

6

Developing Effective Study Skills

Developing appropriate study methods is an important factor in becoming a successful student. This chapter is written for students. Students who are instructed in effective study habits comprehend more material and do better on tests. Students who possess good study habits will likely enjoy school and the challenge of learning. Study skills are methods for solving learning problems. Students who have confidence in their learning skills are able to cope with homework assignments. Students who review the following suggestions will improve their study habits.

Students often not only don't know how to study, but do not know what is important to study. They have to learn how to study and deal with the information they receive in their classes. Learning to learn is an essential component of the learning process. The following study skills outline will provide an overview of the study process:

Study Skills

Preview Material

A general overview of the information can be acquired by reading the table of contents, the chapter titles, the headings, the captions under the pictures, and the summaries.

Summarize Material

Briefly read over the chapter or material and jot down the main ideas. Relate what you have read to homework assignments.

Read Material

Thoroughly read the entire chapter or printed material. While reading, look for the answers to the questions assigned in homework. At the end of each section, review and think about what you have just read.

Take Notes

Underlining, highlighting or taking notes is helpful and summarizes pertinent information to be learned. Taking notes during class lectures or from printed material is an excellent study habit. Notes should be brief and in your own words.

Remember What You Study

Concentrate on what you have just read and learned. After reviewing your notes and important facts several times, try to associate one fact with another. Reread material you don't understand or have forgotten. Jot down main ideas or words on cards and review them in the car, on the way to school, or in your spare time.

Test Yourself

Test yourself by covering your notes and making up questions from them. Try to answer each of the questions and then check the answers for correctness by reading through your notes. In this way, you can decide for yourself which sections of the material need more review and which have been learned.

Improving Reading

When developing effective study habits, improving reading skills is important in becoming a successful students. Some students may have poor reading skills and probably could learn to read faster and more accurately than they do. There are many different reasons for reading in the classroom. The ones that are used the most in classrooms are reading for directions, reading to complete assignments, and reading to prepare for tests. When reading material that is assigned in class, it should be read carefully and slowly. To read textbooks quickly while attempting to comprehend main ideas, dates and statistics is absurd. When reading complex and highly technical material, it is better to slow down and read the material carefully and deliberately. Many textbooks are written in a technical fashion and are difficult to read. It is easy to forget within very short periods of time much of what is read unless it has meaning. You do not always comprehend as you read. Various thoughts presented in textbook chapters, often may seem confusing and overwhelming. In order to become a successful student, you must sort out the material and understand the meaning of words and concepts. While reading a passage, you must decode the printed words and become familiar with the author's intent. You need to become an active and involved reader when completing reading assignments.

When reading to follow directions, you must understand the key words and their meanings. Your responses to the meaning of the words will directly relate to your actions. In order to perform the tasks required in the directions, you need to be able to read and interpret the directions accurately. Another reason for reading in the classroom is to complete assignments. Reading to locate facts and details in a passage is the skill most widely used in completing homework assignments. Teachers often will request that you complete the answers to questions at the end of specific chapters. In order to complete assignments like these, you will have to read the chapter to locate the facts and details that will provide the answers to the questions. Another purpose for reading is preparing for tests. When preparing for tests, you should read the material closely in order to understand the important ideas. You must also be able to recall information and state it in your own words without referring to the text.

When you have a reading assignment, there are several steps you must consider to become more effective:

1. Skim the material to get an overview of what the information is about. Check titles, table of contents, headings, illustrations, and summary statements.
2. Read through the material. Pay close attention to introductory paragraphs and summaries. Ask yourself what significance this material has and why the material is important. Distinguish between relevant and irrelevant information and separate knowledge from opinion.
3. Recognize and understand the facts and details presented in the text and be able to determine the main ideas.
4. Use the dictionary to help you define unfamiliar words. Use context clues to get the meaning of other words.
5. Underline or highlight key words and sentences. Place marks such as asterisks or stars in the margin to identify important ideas. You might want to jot down main ideas and factual information that will be useful at a later time. Outlining chapters is often useful when studying for tests.
6. Go back and scan the material to find specific answers to questions. Rather than read every word in the passage, review the material by scanning it until you find the key words that answer questions. It is not always necessary to read every word in a passage. Look for key words or phrases while you let your eyes run over the material. Pay particular attention to headings and italicized words that will give you clues as to the location of the information you are seeking.
7. Draw inferences from the material you read. Attempt to identify relationships and determine the author's perspective. Draw conclusions about what the author is saying.
8. Summarize what you read in your own words to show that you have fully comprehended the meaning. Paraphrasing helps you make "sense" of the material. Go back over significant sections in the chapters and review key words, definitions, titles, dates, and main ideas.

Preparing for Tests

A major way for teachers to measure how much students have learned is through testing. In order to pass a test, you must master large amounts of information and recall it accurately during a test. Preparing early for tests will eliminate cramming the night before. By scheduling study times for tests, you will be able to plan sufficient study time to review chapters, notes, and study sheets in an organized fashion.

Test taking is one of the most important skills required of students. Many students worry too much about tests and examinations. Often this worry can be so intense, it can cause you to avoid studying or to forget what you have learned. Below are tips on how to study for tests:

Test Taking Tips

1. Try to complete class projects and reports early and have all assignments completed prior to the time of the test.
2. Allow at least seven hours of sleep the night before a test. Do not stay up all night to cram for a test. Cramming tends to increase anxiety, which in turn interferes with your ability to study.
3. Study your notes and texts frequently so that you can spend a couple of days before the test reviewing the material. Real learning occurs through study that is spaced over a period of a few days.
4. If you don't understand some of the material, ask for assistance. The best time to do this is a few days prior to the test.
5. Review all of the material over a period of a few days or weeks. Reviewing includes understanding the information, relating the information to what is already known, and summarizing the material.
6. Read the test directions carefully. If you do not understand the directions, ask the teacher to explain them.
7. Look over the entire examination briefly to see what types of questions are included and the number of points for each question. As you quickly read the questions, make notes in the margin that will assist you in answering the questions. Items worth more points should be given more time to complete.
8. Begin answering the easiest questions first. Do not waste time on objective tests such as matching, true/false, or multiple choice by worrying over questions for which you do not know the answers. If you do not know the answer, it is better to skip the question, placing a mark next to it to identify it, and go on to the next question. If there is time remaining at the end of the test, go back to the unanswered questions.
9. Find out if there is a penalty for "guessing." If there is a penalty for guessing, do not make wild guesses; if you cannot answer the question, leave the space blank. If there is no penalty for guessing, nothing should be left blank. Sometimes a list score is based solely on the number of correct answers; on other tests, however, points are taken off for wrong answers.

Essay Tests

1. Don't leave studying for an essay test until the night before the test. Review all class notes several days before the test and read and review selected chapters in the textbook. The night before the test, review your notes and important

information and get a good night's sleep. Try to feel well prepared and confident when you take the test.

2. Read the directions carefully. If you do not understand them, ask for assistance. Underline key words in the directions such as define, compare and analyze.

3. After skimming all the questions in the test, begin with the question you know best.

4. Carefully budget your time. Although you should begin with the easiest question first, make sure you have time to complete all of the questions. Keep an eye on the clock to help pace yourself. If one question is allotted more points than another, answer it in a more complete fashion. It is often efficient to outline answers to assist you in organizing and sequencing your responses. If time is running out, put down as much information as possible in the time remaining. Most teachers will give partial credit for demonstrating knowledge of the answer.

5. Respond concisely to each question. Write in a clear, legible form. Use complete sentences to answer questions. Answer each question directly, stating your strongest points first. Support your ideas with appropriate examples. Leave space between paragraphs and, if you have time add additional information.

6. Read back through your answers. Make note of misspelled words, incorrect grammar, omitted words and unclear sentences. Add words or phrases to help clarify meaning of sentences. Be sure the teacher can read your answers. Many teachers subtract points for incorrect spelling and grammar errors.

Planning for Long Term Projects

You will be required to participate in long term projects many times throughout a school year. Examples of long term projects might include book reports, science projects, posters, or term papers. Also included are weekly spelling words or chapter assignments. These projects may be assigned a month or several weeks ahead of due dates. The following tips will help you effectively manage long term projects:

Long Term Project Tips

1. No matter how easy the assignment, don't wait until the night before it is due to complete it. There is no way of predicting how much other homework you will have the night before a long term project is due.

2. Since many long term assignments will require outside resources, planning ahead will minimize last minute frustrations because you were unable to acquire the material.

3. Decide what materials you will need to complete the assignment and obtain those materials the first night the project is assigned.

4. Avoid procrastination. Don't put an assignment off because you think it will be too easy or too difficult. Complete a small amount of work on the project each night. At the end of each evening, review what you have accomplished and plan the next evening's work.

5. On the last evening put the project together and proofread it. Ask a friend to review the final draft. Store your final project in a folder or secure container.

Writing a Paper

Writing may include a wide variety of assignments such as term papers, book reports, research reports, themes, essays and summaries. As you progress in school, written assignments require polish and sophistication. In order to continue to improve you should develop effective writing behavior.

An organized plan will help improve your writing skills. The following guidelines will assist you in organizing your writing:

1. Select a topic
2. Develop an outline
3. Use library resources
4. Organize material
5. Compose a rough draft
6. Write a final draft
7. Proofread

Selecting a Topic

Whether you have been assigned a topic by your teacher, or whether you must select your own topic, you need to go through a specific process before you make a final decision about a topic. For you to be enthusiastic about writing, you should be interested in the topic. Begin by visiting the library and reviewing various topic areas of interest to you. After the library visit, the following procedures can be implemented:

1. List possible topics that interest you.
   A.
   B.
   C.
   D.
   E.
2. Look at your list and select the two most interesting.
   A.
   B.

3. Review the two topics you have selected, go to the library and research both topics. Write down two main ideas for each topic.
   A. Topic One
      1.
      2.
   B. Topic Two
      1.
      2.
4. Select one of the topic areas and jot down questions to which you want to know the answer. These questions will give you a starting place when planning your writing. After you have selected a topic, you are ready to outline the material.

Outlining the Paper

An outline is a logical classification of material into main groups and subgroups according to a plan of organization. Think of an outline as a guide that will help you organize the main points you want to make and support those ideas with details needed to clarify the information. Once you have decided on the general topic area, think about what points need to be made first, second and third to clarify the topic area. Decide which points are the most important and use those as the main topic areas. Use ideas and examples to make the information clear to the reader. Examples show what you mean by giving evidence and other specific details. The more thought that is given to organizing and sequencing the facts, the easier writing will become. A beginning outline should be a tentative, working outline. Outlines should be flexible and changeable.

A popular method of outlining is to use numbers and letters to designate topic areas. The main ideas become the main topics in the outline format. By creating an outline, you can change and modify the original format prior to actually writing the paper.

Outline Format

I   Introduction
    A. Subtopic
        1.
        2.
    B. Subtopic
        1.
        2.
II Body of paper
    A. Subtopic
        1.
        2.
    B. Subtopic
        1.
        2.

III Conclusion
   A.   Subtopic
       1.
       2.
   B.   Subtopic
       1.
       2.

Using Library Resources

Papers that provide factual information about certain topics usually require doing library research. Some of the resources available in the library include encyclopedias, journals, magazines, books, almanacs, and other reference materials. Once you have selected your topic, a visit to the library is in order. The people who work in libraries will answer questions about your specific research area. Tell the librarian exactly what you are looking for and feel free to discuss the topic of your paper. Becoming familiar with your library will make your job of research much easier.

You first stop will probably be in the general reference section of the library. Here you will find dictionaries, encyclopedias and handbooks. Your next stop will be at the card catalog. This section will help you locate material pertaining to your topic area that is housed in the library. It is in this area where you will locate current books. Use the periodical section to assist you in locating the most current articles that support your topic area.

If you use materials in the library that you will cite in your paper, be sure to record the title, author's name and other bibliographical information. Using index cards will help you organize your reference materials. Take notes from the material and write them in your own words on the cards. These cards can be color coded for different topic areas. Label each card with a specific heading and record appropriate information on the card. All important information on specific topics should be clustered together.

Organizing Material

Unorganized information is useless. Since unorganized information is useless, you need to organize your material as you gather it. Organization involves classifying facts and material into a logical pattern so that it can be clearly understood by the reader. The information collected on the index cards should follow the general outline of the paper. Review this information and revise it if it does not support the main thesis of the paper. Your outline can serve as a guide when writing an organized paper. It also will help you to put the facts and information you have collected into some order. Go through your index cards and sort them according to the topics of your outline. Once sorted according to topics, sort each pile according to the importance of the information on each card. The first stack of cards should identify the purpose of your paper and introduce the topic to the reader. Arrange the information so that you can state your main idea as simply as possible. The body of the paper comes next. The body is the most important part of the paper because it is where you use the information you have collected to support your thesis statement. Remember to use current books and statistics and relay the information in detail. You are now ready for the conclusion. It should include summary information. Summarize the paper in such a way that it gives suggestions and final recommendations.

Composing the Draft

You are now ready to begin writing the rough draft of your paper. Before you begin writing this first draft, review the outline and make any changes you find necessary. Arrange to have all of the material you will need at your desk. This material would include index cards, outline format, reference materials, dictionary, paper and pencils. Plan to write in large blocks of time. Once you start writing, try not to stop for small interruptions. You will probably accomplish more if you are able to write for an hour or two at a time. Composing the rough draft will be a process of trying ideas out, changing them, throwing some away and keeping others. Your first draft will be messy and appear unorganized. Writing notes in the margins will help you in the writing of the final draft. Try to follow your outline, but don't worry if once you start writing, natural changes occur. Write spontaneously. You can always go back and complete phrases and sentences after you have completed your thoughts. Cross out and change words that are inconsistent and unclear. Give the reader all the information he needs to understand the concepts introduced.

Clearly written sentences assist in clarifying the main idea of your writing. They should be complete, clear, direct and communicative. All sentences must have both a subject and a predicate. Readability is improved when you vary the length of sentences and vary the words used in the sentences. Variety makes for easy and interesting reading.

Sentences are clustered together to form paragraphs. The paragraph is considered a unit of thinking. It contains a group of related sentences written in a logical sequence. When you write, think in clusters of thoughts and combine these clusters of thoughts into paragraphs. Each paragraph should have a topic sentence which emphasizes your main point in the paragraph. The topic sentence should be presented in a unified, coherent manner. The important ideas about this topic should be developed by stating, explaining and comparing thoughts. Good paragraphs have sentences in them that are arranged in logical order. The central idea should be presented first and secondary thoughts should support the main idea. The supportive sentences make the reader understand what you are trying to say. They define terms and explain the ideas in detail. Avoid unnecessary repetition of words and ambiguity in sentences. Careful writers do not use words which their readers may misinterpret. They write sentences that are understandable.

The length of the paragraphs is determined by the purpose and the importance of the ideas presented. If the central idea is complex, the paragraph will be long in order to define and illustrate what the idea means. All sentences in a paragraph should relate directly to the main idea of the paragraph. Although you should use words that the reader knows, certain terms that are familiar to you may be unknown to the reader. Define all technical words immediately after you use them. Do not assume that words used in context will give the reader an accurate definition. Even commonly used words should be defined in the text. To clarify sentences, all words should be understood by the reader after the passage has been read.

Rewriting the Draft

As you write over a period of time, you develop certain phrases and words which are called in writing your "style." You should try to develop an effective and readable style to improve writing and understanding. Pay particular attention to your style of writing when you begin the rewriting process.

It is usually easier to rewrite the draft rather than attempt to correct it. The rough draft is often so full of corrections and deletions that it is hard to read. When you are rewriting, be aware of proofreading guidelines and pay particular attention to spelling errors. Check to see if your wording is concise and that were carefully selected. If your sentences are choppy or too long, rewrite them.

Retype the final draft on white bond paper that is easy to correct. When you have finished the draft of the paper, set it aside for a day or two. Look at it again to see if it captures the main ideas and informs the reader about the topic in a simple, well sequenced way.

Proofreading

Many errors on papers are the result of carelessness. These problems usually relate to spelling, punctuation and grammar. Your final paper should be as neat and accurate as you can make it. Carefully check for spelling errors by using a dictionary. A paper that is correct is more effective than one with errors in it. Before handing in your paper, proofread it by following these steps:

1. Check the form of the paper.
   A. Is the paper well organized?
   B. Is the paper clear?
   C. Is the general appearance of the paper neat?
2. Check the content of the paper.
   A. Are the ideas presented in a sequenced way?
   B. Did you use examples adequately?
   C. Have you defined technical words?
   D. Have you summarized the paper?
3. Check the style of the paper.
   A. Have you used the most appropriate language and paragraph structure?
   B. Did you capitalize and punctuate correctly?
   C. Did you correct spelling errors?

Proofread every page you type. It is sometimes easier to find errors if you read the paper out loud. Make your corrections neatly. Some errors can be corrected by erasing or covering the mistake with liquid paper. If a page contains several corrections, it should be retyped. Most teachers prefer papers that are corrected neatly.

Make an effort to give the final paper an attractive appearance. Use good quality paper. Widely acceptable is white bond paper measuring 8 1/2 x 11 inches. Erasers and ink eradicators work well on this type of paper. All papers should be typewritten on one side of the sheet and double spaced. A black typewriter ribbon is easy to read and unlikely to fade. When typing the paper, margins often vary and students should check with the teacher to be certain of typing requirements. All pages should be numbered from first to last page. Numbers are placed in the upper right corner of each page. If the format requires a title page, select a title that is clear and descriptive.

Using the Library

Many resources are available in the library. Libraries are filled with books, encyclopedias and other reference material. Libraries also have journals, magazines, newspapers and audiovisual material.

Resource Material

Fiction Books

Fiction books are used for recreational reading. They are arranged on the shelves in alphabetical order according to the authors' last names.

Nonfiction Books

Nonfiction books contain facts and information. These books are divided into number groups and are arranged on the shelves by numbers which are clearly seen on the backs of the books as they stand upright on the shelves. The numbers, along with the first two letters of the author's name, is referred to as the "call number." These numbers help locate books on the shelves.

Reference Books

Reference books are located in a special section of the library. Reference material includes dictionaries and encyclopedias. Students frequently use encyclopedias which are usually found on special shelves in the library. These books focus in on people, places, things, and events all over the world. Generally, articles in encyclopedias are arranged alphabetically. Dictionaries and almanacs are useful for providing information about words and finding specific facts or details about subjects or people. The information in almanacs is updated each year and the subjects are listed alphabetically.

Periodical and Printed Material

Journals, magazines and newspapers of all kinds are kept in the library. They are called periodical literature, and have up - to-date facts on many subjects. The best way to find a magazine with specific information is to look in the Reader's Guide. Pamphlets, clippings and government publications are also included in this area. Each library has a list of the periodicals it keeps in stock.

Audiovisual Materials

Audiovisual materials include films, slides, records, tapes, maps, globes, microfilm, computers and computer software. This material is housed in a designated audiovisual area and the equipment necessary to use the material is stored nearby.

Resources in the Library

Card Catalog Area

The card catalog is an index of all the materials in the library and the locations where these materials can be found. It is housed in a cabinet with many small drawers which are labeled from A to Z. For each book, there are three cards in the card catalog. The subject card has the subject or topic of the book written at the top of the card. A subject card is made for each subject that is discussed fully in a book. The title card has the title of the book across the top of the card. Under the name of the book, the author's name is typed. The author card has the author's name at the top, with the last name written first. The author card gives the author's full name, date of birth, the title of the book, the place of publication, publisher and the date of publication. All cards have the call number of the book in the upper left hand corner. Many libraries are currently using a computer cataloging system for locating materials in the library. The computer monitor displays the information traditionally stored in the card catalog. Although each system operates differently, all systems use the same three classifications and give all the information found in the card catalog.

Reference Area

This section in the library is an area designated where reference works such as dictionaries, encyclopedias, indexes and directories are housed. Reference material usually can not be checked out and is used within the area.

Classification System

Most libraries store materials using the Library of Congress classification system. This system uses letters of the alphabet for broad categories and numbers for finer divisions. The Library of Congress Classification system follows.

A   General works
    AC   collections
    AE   encyclopedias
    AY   yearbooks
    AZ   general history

B Philosophy-religion
  BC logic
  BF psychology
  BL religions

C History-auxiliary sciences
  CB civilization
  CS genealogy
  CT biography

D History and topography
  DA Great Britain
  DC France
  DK Russia
  DU Australia and Oceania

E-F America
  E   America and United States - general
  F   United States local and America except the United States

G Geography
  GC oceanography
  GN anthropology
  GT manners and customs
  GV sports and amusements

G Social sciences
  HB economic theory
  HD economic history
  HE transportation
  HF commerce
  HG finance
  HM sociology
  HQ family
  HT communities
  HV social pathology, philanthropy

J Political science
  JA general works
  JO theory of the state
  JX international law

K Law

L Education
  LB theory and practice
  LC special forms
  LD United States

M Music
  ML literature of music
  MT musical instruction

N Fine Arts
  NA architecture
  ND painting
  NK industrial arts

P Language and literature
  PA classical languages
  PC romance languages
  PD Teutonic languages
  PR English literature
  PS American literature

Q science
  QA mathematics
  QC physics
  QD chemistry
  QE geology
  QL zoology
  QP physiology

R Medicine
  RB pathology
  RE ophthalmology
  RK dentistry
  RM therapeutics
  RT nursing

S Agriculture -plant and animal industry
  SB plant culture
  SD forestry
  SF animal culture
  K hunting sports

T T chnology
  T engineering
  TH building construction
  TK electrical engineering
  TN mineral industries
  TR photography

U Military science

V Naval science

Z Bibliography and Library Science

Summary

This chapter has reviewed effective study techniques. The chapter was written to outline successful study strategies for the students. Successful students regularly practice good study skills. They study every day, even though they might not have a definite homework assignment. When practicing good study habits, students need to develop skills in reading, writing, notetaking, organizing time, taking tests and using the library. Students will improve study habits by practicing study skills reviewed in this chapter. Once you realize that developing effective study habits involves using these skills, you will improve the effectiveness of your study time. Developing good work habits requires that you have a positive attitude about completing assignments. Realize that in order to improve, you must not only feel good about school, but feel confident about your ability to successfully completing the assignments. scheduling your day helps you keep on the right track. Set up a realistic and workable schedule that allows you to earmark time for both work and play. Your schedule needs to be one that allows for a variety of activities, while maintaining a schedule for regular home study. The study skills discussed in this chapter should enable you to become a better learner.

References

Anderson, R. H. *Selecting and developing media for instruction.* New York: Van Nostrand Reinhold Co., 1976.

Asante, M. K., & Frye, J. K. *Contemporary public communication: Applications.* New York: Harper & Row Publishers, 1977.

Azumi J., & Madhere S. Characteristics of high achieving elementary schools in Newark. *Newark School District Research Report* (ORET Report No. 5). Newark Board of Education, Newark: Office of Research, Evaluation and Testing, 1982.

Barber, B. Homework does not belong on the agenda for educational reform. *Educational Leadership,* 43, 1986, 55-57.

Barker, L. L. *Communication in the classroom.* Englewood Cliffs: Prentice-Hall,1982.

Bedwell, L. E., Hunt, G. H., Touzel, T. J., & Wiseman, D. G. *Effective teaching.* Springfield: Charles C.Thomas, 1984.

Berger, E. H. *Parents as partners.* Columbus: Merrill, 1987.

Bond, G. W., & Smith, G. J. Homework in the elementary school. *National Elementary Principal,* 45, 1966, 46-50.

Bossert, S. T. *Tasks and social relationships in classrooms.* Cambridge: Cambridge University Press, 1979.

Bower, S. A. *Painless public speaking.* New Jersey: Prentice-Hall, 1981.

Brainerd, C. J. (Ed.) & Pressley, M. (Ed.) *Basic processes in memory development.* New York: Springer-Verlag, 1985.

Christen, W. L., & Murphy, T. J. How important are study skills? *NASSP Bulletin,* October, 1985, 82-88.

Clemes, H., & Bean, R. *Self esteem: The key to your child's well being.* New York: G. P. Putnam's sons, 1981.

Corner, J. (Ed.) & Hawthorn,J. (Ed.) *Communication studies: An introductory reader.* Great Britain: Edward Arnold, 1985.

Cuban, L. *Teachers and machines.* New York: Teachers College Press, 1986.

Davies, I. K. *The management of learning.* New York: McGraw Hill, 1971.

Davies, I. K. *Instructional Technique.* New York: McGraw-Hill, 1981.

Devine, T. G. *Teaching study skills.* Boston: Allyn & Bacon, 1981.

Emmer, E. T., Evertson, C. M., Sanford, J. P., Clements, B. S., & Worsham, M. E. *Classroom management for secondary teachers.* Englewood Cliffs: Prentice-Hall, 1984.

England, D. A., & Flatley, J. K. *Homework—and why. Library of Congress Catalog, Card Number 84-62988, 1985.*

Feldman, R. S. (Ed.) *The social psychology of education.* Cambridge: Cambridge University Press, 1986.

Green, J., & Brown, R. *Student achievement in public and private schools.* Denver: Education Commission of the States, 1983.

Hahn, J. *Have you done your homework?* New York: John Wiley and Sons, 1985.

Harris, M. T. *How to be successful in reading, studying, taking exams, and writing in college.* Warminster: Surrey Press, 1983.

Howell, R. W., & Vetter, H. J. *Language and behavior.* (2nd Ed.) New York: Human Sciences Press, 1985.

Kail, R. *The development of memory in children.* (2nd. Ed.) New York: W.H. Freeman & Co., 1984.

Karoly, P., (Ed.) Steffen, J. J. *Improving Children's Competence.* Livingston: D. C. Heath, 1982.

Kelly, E. A. *Improving school climate.* Reston: National Association of Secondary School Principals, 1980.

Kerzic, R. L. *Value of homework.* The Clearing House, 1966, 41, 140-142.

Knorr, C. L. *A synthesis of homework research and related literature.* Paper presented to Lehigh Chapter of Phi Delta Kappa, Eric document Ed 199933, 1981.

LaConte, R. T. *Homework as a learning experience: What research says to the teacher.* Washington, D. C.: National Education Association, 1981.

Levy-Leboyer, C. *Psychology and environment.* Beverly Hills: Sage Publishers, 1982.

Lee, J. R., & Pruitt, K. W. *Homework assignments: Classroom games or teaching tools?* Clearing House, 1979, 53, 31-35.

Loughlin, C. E., & Suina, J. H. *The learning environment.* New York: Teachers College Press, 1982.

Madsen, C. H., & Madsen, C. K. *Teaching/discipline: A positive approach for educational development.* (3rd. Ed.) Boston: Allyn & Bacon, 1981.

Mikulas, W. L. *Concepts in learning.* Philadelphia: W. B. Sanders, 1974.

Molloy, J. T. *The woman's dress for success book.* New York: Warner Books, 1977.

Molloy, J. T. *Live for success.* New York: William Morrow, 1981.

Paine, S. C., Radicchi, J. A., Rosellini, L. C., Deutchman, L., & Darch, C. B. *Structuring your classroom for academic success.* Champaign: Research Press, 1983.

Patton, J. E., Stinard, T., & Routh, D. Where do children study? *The Educational Digest,* February, 1984.

Pressley, M. (Ed.) & Brainerd, C. J. (Ed.) *Cognitive learning and memory in children.* New York: Springer-Verlag, 1985.

Purkey, S. C., & Smith, M. S. *Highlights from research on effective schools.* Alexandria: Association for Supervision and Curriculum Development, 1982.

Purkey, W. W. *Inviting school success.* Belmont: Wadsworth, 1978.

Roths, L. E. *Teaching for learning.* Columbus: Charles E. Merrill, 1969.

Rothwell, J. D., & Costigan, J. I. *Interpersonal communication.* Columbus: Charles Merrill, 1975.

Shea, G. F. *Managing a difficult or hostile audience.* Englewood Cliffs: Prentice-Hall, 1984.

Sleeman, P. J., & Rockwell, D. M. *Designing learning environments.* New York: Longman, 1981.

Stanford, G., & Roark, A. E. *Human interaction in education.* Boston: Allyn & Bacon, 1974.

Suydam, M. D. Homework: Yes or no? *Arithmetic Teacher,* 1985, 32, 56.

Tillman, M. *Trouble-shooting classroom problems.* Glenview: Scott, Foresman, 1986.

Walberg, H. J. Families as partners in educational productivity. *Phi Delta Kappan,* 1984, 65, 397-400.

Walberg, H. J., Paschal, R. S., & Weinstein, T. Homework's powerful effects on learning. *Educational Leadership,* 1985, 42, 76-79.

Walberg, H. J., Paschal, R. A., & Weinstein, T. Walberg and colleagues reply: Effective schools use homework effectively. *Educational Leadership,* 1986, 43, 58.

U. S. Department of Education. *What works: Research about teaching and learning.* Washington, D. C.: U. S. Department of Education, 1986.

Walker, M. *Writing research papers.* New York: W. W. Norton, 1987.

Wilkinson, L. C. *Communicating in the classroom.* New York: Academic Press, 1982.

Wood, J. A. School based homework assistance, *Educational Horizons,* 1986, 64, 99-101.

Ziebell, D., & Check, J. How to make effective homework assignments. *The Educational Digest.* December, 1980.